Yes

By

Maria Orrù

In Dedication to Yeshua

Thank you, Yeshua, for your wisdom and love!

"The Kingdom of God is inside you and all around you, Not in a mansion of wood and stone. Split a piece of wood and God is there, Lift a stone and you will find God."

— From the film Stigmata

The photos in this book are authentic photos of our spiritual self after we leave the material body behind.

CHAPTERS

YESHUA

The Soul

When it comes to the soul, there is a great deal of things that both contradicts itself and is difficult to understand. I would like to define these three essential stages of our life by defining them for you, and we will begin with a spiritual being. I will begin by defining those stages for you. In addition, I shall examine the human being and the spiritual being in greater detail. When a spiritual being is also referred to as a spirit, what is the explanation behind this phenomenon. Yahweh, the Father, Mother, and Creator of all life forms, is the one who created us all. At our heart, we are all pure spirit beings, and with the creative force of love, we bring out the spiritual life forms out of the light that is constantly flowing. During this lesson, we will acquire an understanding of the process of spiritual evolution, which entails the slow evolution of the fertilised spiritual atom from the realm of ethereal minerals. After that, one arrives at the ethereal plant kingdom, then the ethereal animal kingdom, then the ethereal nature spirit kingdom, and finally, one arrives at an ethereal spirit being that is whole and resplendent in its fullness. Whoever is a son or daughter of Yahweh, is complete and eternal. A large number of these pure spirit beings, which we might also refer to as angels, left the immaculate heavens just a short time after the beginning of creation. This unfortunate event occurred not long after the beginning of existence. This occurred as a result of their self-will or selfishness, in addition to their desire to be like Yahweh. The concepts of love, tenderness, and kindness were not ones that they were willing to consider embracing. This event, which is referred to as the fall in the Bible, occurred when they got the belief that they could make something that was superior to what Yahweh had created. These divine spirit beings descended into the lower spiritual and fine material cosmos that were located outside of the pure heavens as a result of the fact that they were no longer able to withstand the high selfless love vibration that was present in the few heavens. Additionally, these worlds are sometimes referred to as fall worlds. They had a strong sense of self-will, they were absolutely opposed to the will of Yahweh, who is love, and they created layer upon layer of negativity surrounding their original, pure essence. They have created a very negative environment for themselves. These layers are visible to us in the same way that we are able to differentiate between the layers of an onion. Additionally, these layers are referred to as soul clothing, and from this point forward, these entities will be referred to as souls, which is a term that refers to a spirit being that is burdened. One might say that the soul is a delicate material structure that contains the essence of the original spirit that was present in the soul throughout its existence. It is impossible to find a way to corrupt the soul because it is the sacred spark of the spirit. Furthermore, the spark is referred to as Yahweh's spark in certain references. It is via this component that the soul is able to retain a direct connection with Yahweh, our Father, and it is also through this component that the soul is able to receive the divine life energy. As a consequence of the fall, the original, divine vitality that was contained inside the soul has been considerably depleted, which is the reason for its manifestation. If the soul did not have this link to the spirit of Yahweh, it would be unable to continue existing. Only then would it be able to continue existing. The negative energy that was responsible for the construction of these soul garments is what we would refer to as our sins, which are also known as our karmic duties. In order for us to be able to return to our eternal home, which is the heavens that are pure, it will, at some time in the future, have to be transformed back into love. There was an increase in the amount of destruction, exploitation, power, hunger, limitations, degeneration, mutilations, coldness, death, and darkness that was brought about by the negativity of these souls over the course of time. Because of this negativity, the layers of the soul got more rigid, and their surrounds also became more rigid. Their surroundings likewise became more rigid. In the beginning of the osmosis process, the planets were directly influenced by the continuous negative radiation that these materials emitted, which led to the introduction of the process. Over the course of more than one million years, which is an unfathomably lengthy period of time, this is how the material osmosis evolved. We must not forget that there is no such thing as the solidity of stuff. This is something that we must keep in mind. This entire region outside of pure heaven is now referred to as the purification fields. This is due to the fact that many of these fallen souls have since come to the realisation that they were wrong in the beginning and are now working on themselves in order to return to the eternal home that is Yahweh. This is due to the fact that a significant number of these souls have spent time and effort improving themselves. For this, they have to walk from level to level and experience their karmic burdens, they are so dominant until those souls have become unconditional, unlimited, and all-inclusive, selfless love again to enter the pure heavens according to the law of light attracts like and facing our own karmic burdens, also called sins that we have created, can be very slow and painful in these fine material worlds of the purification spheres. In spite of this, many of us were granted the extraordinary opportunity to incarnate onto planet Earth into a physical human form for a very brief and intense period of time. This was done in order to speed up the process. As a consequence of this, the

3

soul that has now become embodied in a physical human body is referred to as a human being. This is precisely what you and I are at this very moment. In our day-to-day existence, we, as human beings, have the goal of dissolving our karma, which is also referred to as our soul layers. This can be accomplished by showing love to others and providing service to others without expecting anything in return. Additionally, this covers the act of forgiving, expressing regret, begging forgiveness, and avoiding from making the same mistakes again and again. Because of this, our pure spirit, which is reflected in our soul, is able to shine through us once more. This is a consequence of this. After our physical deaths, our souls will be drawn to the realm that corresponds to it vibrationally, and the manner in which we have lived our lives here on Earth will influence the domain to which our souls will be drawn during this process. We shall be drawn to a higher level from the material realms, and we will be drawn closer to the pure heavens, if we have made the most of our time here on Earth. If we have done this, we will be transferred to a higher level. In the event that this does not take place, we shall be attracted to a lower level that revolves around the Earth. The principle of attraction states that similar things attract one another, and this principle applies to everything. From the most fundamental point of view, each and every one of us is a divine son or daughter of Yahweh, a spirit being or spiritual being that is pristine and unblemished. This first stage is what is meant to be conveyed by the text in the Bible that declares that everyone of us is created in the image of Yahweh. Therefore, it is not the humans who were formed in the image of Yahweh; rather, it is our first ideal state of being in the heavens that encompassed the beginning of our existence before we were created. Is it possible for us to acknowledge the difference that emerged as a consequence of the fall. This pure spirit being entered the sphere of cause and effect and transformed into a soul, which is a spirit that is surrounded by soul burdens, which are also referred to as karma. During the process of incarnation, this soul gets the opportunity to spend a brief but significant amount of time here on Earth as a human being. Within the shortest amount of time possible, the major objective of this time is to alleviate the karmic burden that it has collected.

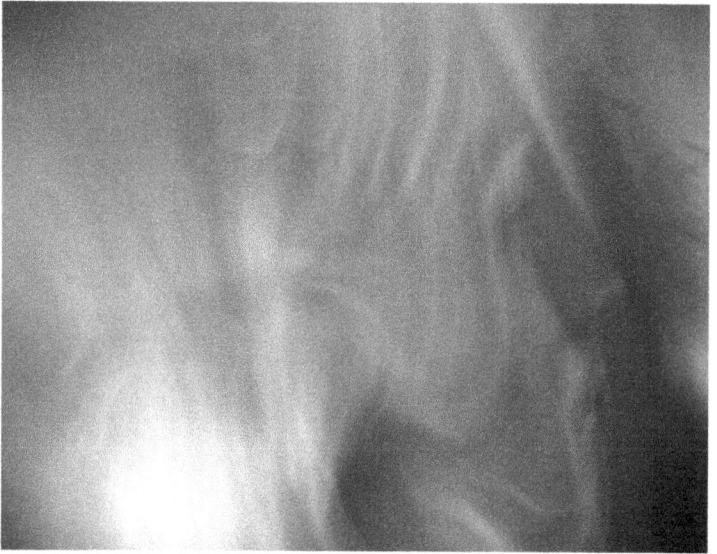

Those born in the flesh cannot see the kingdom of
Yahweh. Christ has risen and only can be seen when the
eyes no longer dwell on the flesh.

(John 3:3)

YESHUA

Christ Spark

You have to go all the way back to the very beginning of creation, and here you will find the most powerful and all-encompassing energy, the primordial source from which the Father, Mother Yahweh, the Creator God, emerges. It is from this source that the absolute eternal reality, which is comprised of seven enormous heavens and all of their spiritual life forms, was fashioned. As a result of the mineral plant, animal nature spirits, and spiritual beings, these ethereal heavens, together with the entirety of creation, are continuously growing and developing. In contrast, there was a revolt in the beginning, when things were not quite as complex as they are now. This rebellion was led by a number of spiritual beings or angels. Their commander was Satana, also known as Lucifer, who aspired to be like Yahweh. Others know him as Lucifer. Her objective was to demolish everything that Yahweh had created, and then to establish her own heavens, in which she would rule as God and hold the position of ruler. Therefore, all destructive energies that we currently observe, such as war or terrorism, are the satanic principle. Through the law of attraction and rejection, Satana and her large number of followers were unable to continue existing in the pure love stream of the absolute heavens. As a result, they projected themselves into the outer regions, which eventually became the seven fall spheres that surround the pure heavens. This occurrence is referred to as the "fall of angels." These seven regions are a mirror of the seven fundamental powers that Yahweh possesses, and they are also a reflection of the pure heavens. In addition to order, they are mercy, love, patience, earnestness, wisdom, and the will of the divine. It is said that the lowest four are the four natures of Yahweh, and they are the ones that are the farthest away from the central sun, which is the source of life. The egocentricity and selfishness of these rebellious souls increased as a result of Satana's encouragement. As a result of the fact that many of them burdened themselves more and more, they moved further and further away from the heavens that are pure. A great number of them fell precisely here into the lowest four regions, where they would receive an even smaller amount of life force from the central sun. They proceeded to steal life energies from one another with more vigour in order to maintain their own survival, which resulted in an increase in their karma. This is the most distant field, which encompasses the material or physical universe and includes the planet Earth. Matter is nothing more than light that has been changed into a lower form. The density of these souls eventually resulted in the formation of a physical body here on Earth, where they had fallen to such a great extent. But not a single one of these spirits that had fallen was ever lost. Throughout the entire period, the father, mother, as Yahweh sent messengers, prophets, and wise souls into the fall region in order to request that all of the souls return to their homes. A significant number of these messengers and prophets also travelled to the planet Earth with the intention of convincing the people to abandon their egocentricity and make their way back to love and Heaven. However, the majority of the efforts were for naught. The fallen ones became more and more entangled in their own selfishness, and along with it came a surge in destruction, warfare, and misery. This is precisely what Satan or Lucifer desired, which was to destroy creation. The fallen souls, over the course of aeons and aeons of time, accumulated an increasing amount of karma, which was their own energy, and their access to divine energy was having an effect on their seven energy centres. From the highest crown to the lowest, these energy centres, which the eastern tradition refers to as chakras, are a reflection of Yahweh's seven qualities. These powers are mercy, love, patience, sincerity, wisdom, will, and order, just like the pure heavens. As a result of the immense karmic responsibilities, the seven energy centres of these fallen souls that were circulating at a rapid pace have slowed down to the point where they would finally stop and reverse their rotation. They were on the verge of reaching the very critical tipping point of devolution, which would be the undoing of creation. This would be a slow but unstoppable path back from the spiritual being to the nature spirit, to the animals, the plants, and the minerals, and eventually back into the eternally flowing primordial spirit from which everything had once originated. It would have been impossible to avert the collapse of all spiritual forms and worlds, which would have been the inevitable consequence of the entire equilibrium of creation that would have been thrown out. In that case, Satana or Lucifer would have been successful and would have been able to establish her very own wicked heavens. On the other hand, it was at this cosmic tipping point that an extraordinary event took place, which prevented the oncoming collapse of creation. In order to teach the absolute way of love via the use of examples and lessons, the divine love energy that some people refer to as the son of Yahweh or Christ incarnated into the person that we know as Yeshua incarnated here on Earth. The entire demonic worlds in all of the fallen regions were jolted by this event because it was of such an amazing scale. After a moment of reflection, they realised that their plan of devastation was now in grave danger. Christ came to earth, taught, and walked the road of love that is without limit. The established religious hierarchy, which were already under the influence of the demonic forces at the time, were subjected to stringent criticism from him. Subsequently, these demonic powers utilised all of their power and influence, and with the support of the priesthood, they were able to convince the populace to have Christ crucified. It is not a karmic event that Christ was crucified and killed in such a horrible manner. The Satanic or Luciferian powers made a last-ditch effort to thwart his purpose, but nothing was successful. Christ came to the realisation that his mission to transform the minds and hearts of all souls through the transmission of his teachings and the example he set was doomed to fail. Having exhausted all other possibilities, he ultimately made the decision to sacrifice himself for the children of Yahweh who had fallen and had departed from heaven. It was on the cross that Christ said the words "It is finished." He gave of himself at that moment. He extracted from the greatest, endlessly flowing primordial potential, the spirit of love, and implanted it as sparks into all of the souls of the four lower purification spheres. These souls had severely burdened themselves by violating the law of love, and he implanted it into them as sparks. It was like a massive fireworks display that caused all of the worlds that had been destroyed to shake. This spark became the support and stability for the souls that had fallen, preventing their spirit essence from dissolving back into the spirit that flows endlessly and putting an end to the process. It was no longer possible for the energy centres, often known as chakras, to reserve or reverse themselves. The entire creation was saved for all eternity, and every soul that was carrying an enormous burden was saved by this act of redemption. Since then, everything has been making its way back to Yahweh, the actual fact, and is currently on its journey back home. As a result, Christ became the Redeemer for all souls and persons who had fallen so far below the level of perfection that they had lost their ability to reactivate the four divine rays of consciousness, which are order, divine will, wisdom, and earnestness. It is only until the soul has regained the fourth layer of purification that redemption may be considered effective inside that soul. After that, the energy of this spark of redemption, which has been supporting, upholding, and guiding the soul, returns to the power that was present in the beginning. The soul has then consciously accepted its relationship to Yahweh, and it will enter the drawing force of Yahweh in order to make the final preparations to return to the absolute reality, which is the heart of God. This potent Christ Spark is an additional energy spark that is located in the neighbourhood of our heart and the region of the fourth energy centre. It is a spark that is rich in power. Every soul that has fallen is helped to follow the path of love by it, and it rapidly changes any negativity into love. And how exactly do we go about doing this. He instructed us to always compare our ideas, words, actions, and feelings to the ten Commandments and the sermon on the mount. If we do this, we will immediately know what is not in alignment and what it is that we need to change inside ourselves. Christ taught us to do this. To move on to the next level, we must experience profound regret or remorse for our mistakes and refrain from repeating them. Furthermore, if we have caused harm to another person, we must seek their forgiveness and make restitution. In the same way, we are required to totally forgive anybody and everyone who we believe has caused us damage in any way. If we are hesitant to forgive others, then we cannot come to expect forgiveness from them. The Christ spark will then turn the negative karmic energy into good energy and stream it into our body. This will result in our body being healed from the effects of negative karma, such as an illness. Christ always begins by healing the soul, which then becomes a conduit for the flow of light and power into the physical body. Christ's transformation into the inner physician and healer occurred this way.

The spark is the light that glows brilliantly or dimly within us, depending on how we polish and use it so that it might shine brightly or dimly. Everyone of us possesses a flame that cleanses us. To provide a more in-depth comprehension, I would want to make it clear that the Christ Spark is not the same as the God's spark, which is the divine essence that cannot be corrupted and is present in all sentient beings. This spark is what establishes a direct connection between us and Yahweh. A gift of redemption from Christ, the Christ Spark ensures that every soul that has been lost will eventually find its way back home.

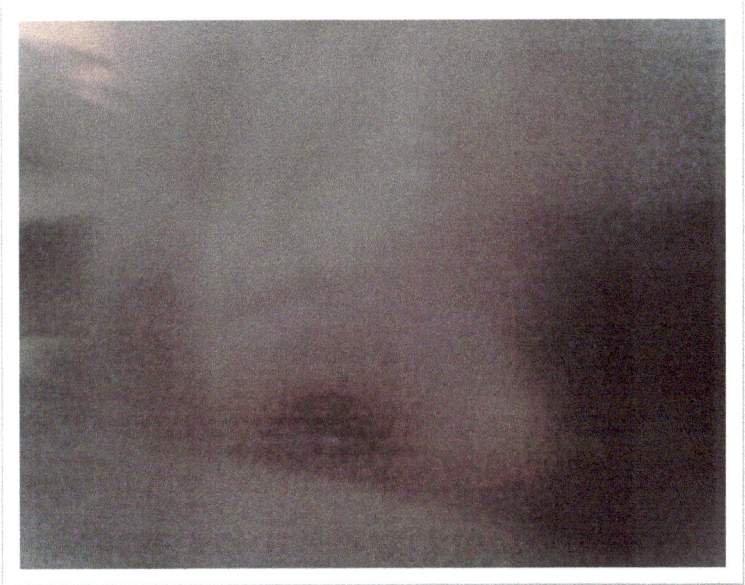

The kingdom of heaven is like these little ones and the
spiritual realm needs those imprisoned in the flesh to heal
the misconceptions of the spiritual realm and to
understand that Yahweh is love. Children are innocent and
pure and need love even in the spiritual form.

(Matthew 5:37)

YESHUA

The Eternal

The eternal and infinite reality is the spiritual cosmos, which is composed of multiple dimensions and contains all of the galaxies, stars, and planets. In addition to being referred to as the pure heavens, it is our spiritual home. Central to this is Yahweh, who is energy and a multidimensional being with consciousness, an unconditionally loving being, filled with life, consciousness, intelligence, and Yahweh's will, which is living in unity with all that is and we, as well as all of creation, are the sunbeams radiating from this heaven, we are created out of the streaming light of Yahweh, just like a sunbeam, so we are not Yahweh, but we are part of Yahweh and we are never separated from Yahweh. In our capacity as these sunbeams, we are the co-creators who fashioned and built the ever-expanding spiritual universes along with them. The fact that we accomplished this in accordance with the will of Yahweh indicates that we were confirming and living the unity with everything that is unconditional love. We also lived in perpetual bliss, ecstasy, or joy, which is our genuine state of being, our essence. We do have polarity, such as up and down and right and left, but we do not have anything that we could consider to be a negative experience, such as war, hatred, agony, or suffering. We are completely amazing, and there is nothing else that can be said about us. This is an absolute reality. The explanation for this is straightforward: Yahweh is the absolute reality, and Yahweh is the absolute reality. Some esoteric traditions tell us that the sun does not need the darkness in order to exist, to define itself, or to feel itself. This is not the case. Yahweh is nothing more than the sun, just way the sun shines. That is all Yahweh is. This is the place where we first established our home, from which we emerged into our actual divine being and the material that we are composed of. The reason that we are not there at this moment is because Yahweh possesses his own free will, and because we are his children, we also possess our own free will. Because we are a part of Yahweh, we always have the option to choose whether we want to follow his will or our own will. Without the ability to exercise our own free will, we would be treated in the same manner as robots, and existence would be devoid of any significant purpose. It was the beginning of the only me, thinking of the egoistic self-willed versus Yahweh's will, and in the scripture, we call this occurrence the fall. Aeons ago, a small group of these sunbeams, which are believed to be spiritual beings, turned away from their source, which was Yahweh, and from the will of Yahweh. They no longer desired to live for the well-being of all, but rather for themselves. It is possible to relate it to a large orchestra in which all of the musicians are playing a lovely and harmonious piece of music together, then all of a sudden, some of the musicians decide to play their own tune. As is only natural, these artists have made the decision to withdraw from their participation in the large orchestra. What happens when we turn away from the light or switch off the light that is constantly flowing through us and providing us with energy. As a result of our turning away from the source of the light, we are essentially filtering it out. The outcome is darkness, a deep dark area in which there is either no light or very little light. We become an impediment that now blocks the light, and the atmosphere is filled with darkness. Due to the fact that we have refused to acknowledge Yahweh, we are now confronted with this darkness, and our initial response to what we see is terror. This is our imagined condition of separation, and with fear, our selfishness increases since everything now becomes an issue of our survival. We certainly believe that we are separated from Yahweh because we are facing away from Yahweh because we have forgotten who we are in reality we have forgotten who we are. The majority of our ideas, according to the claims of some experts, are either directly or indirectly connected to our ability to survive. Due to the fact that we have made the decision to no longer rely on the life energy that comes from Yahweh, the source, we are now required to locate energy that comes from sources that are external to ourselves. There is no better way to convey it than via the course of miracles. This love is the same as energy life force, and the only two actions that are possible in life are offering love and crying out for love. Both of these actions are the only ones that exist. As a result of the fact that we are no longer allowing love to flow through us in order to feed and nourish us, we are now in need of love from one another. Now, life is a never-ending struggle for energy, ranging from the most basic things, such as a want for other people and attention, to more complex things, such as a desire for praise and recognition, to open conflict. We were continuously taking energies, both collectively and individually. this was something that we did. From other people's life force. Every single aggression, every single hate, every single greed, every single lust, every single envy, every single pride, every single battling, and every single suffering are all battles for energy for life force because we feel empty. We have failed to remember that we are living in the boundless riches that is Yahweh's will. The fear of suffering is a product of this darkness that we have produced. Karma is the process by which our bad sentiments, thoughts, and words, as well as our acts, become bullets that we fire at other people. These bullets eventually come back to us as a result of our actions. We carry the weight of our karma on our souls. The more responsibilities we carry, the less divine light can shine through us and nourish us. Additionally, the more darkness we see and experience ahead of us, the more desperate we become for survival. Karma is a barrier for the light, and the more burdens we have, the less divine light can reach us and nourish us. As a result, our objective is to cleanse all of our karma in this location. We accomplish this by forgiving, asking for forgiveness, and refraining from stealing energy from other people through negative emotions, thoughts, words, and actions that are in opposition to the will of Yahweh, which is the will of unity with all or succour unconditional love. This darkness that we have created by obstructing the light that is passing through us is referred to as the relative reality because it is both transient and relative. The light is restored, but the darkness is only momentary. The material universe, which includes our planet Earth, is considered to be one of the four realms that are generally referred to as the temporary four worlds. Despite the fact that we perceive the dimensions of our material cosmos to be enormous, the reality is that it is incredibly small in comparison to the dimensions of our spiritual home. Contrasts are also present in this relative reality that we inhabit. Some people refer to them as dualities, such as good and evil. Those things that we consider to be positive and those that we consider to be negative. Nevertheless, what is good and what is bad? The worldview of Mother Teresa was considerably different from that of Hitler, who believed that what was good for Germany was also harmful. Mother Teresa's vision of what is good was very different. In this relative reality, we all have human judgements, and judgements are always based on our own personal ideas and our own perspective of the world. As a result, some people perceive a terrorist as a cruel person, while others see him as a freedom warrior. Every aspect is relative. It is not enough for us to just avoid doing evil things and perform good things since these are judgements. We want to transcend our dual nature and reclaim our divine nature as our ultimate objective. In order to accomplish this, we must first become fully aware of who we truly are and then live our lives in complete accordance with the will of Yahweh, which is love. To become active for the well-being of all people without any expectations, incentives, or recognition is what it means to engage in this activity. This is also referred to as our going home, or our homecoming, and it occurs when we reverse our karma and turn back towards Yahweh, who is our source, rather than turning away from Yahweh. When we make it possible for the divine light to flow freely through both our spiritual and physical bodies, we will once again be the light, and we will only perceive light again. The darkness that was created will vanish without any further intervention. Enlightenment can be understood in this manner. Allowing light to pass through is what it signifies. There is a challenge for each and every one of us to always keep in mind who we are in fact and to transform our self-centred thinking into a knowledge of the unity that exists within Yahweh. We are fortunate to have a magnificent example to follow, as the highest light that has ever incarnated as the one we call Yeshua has demonstrated to us how to travel the road of divine love.

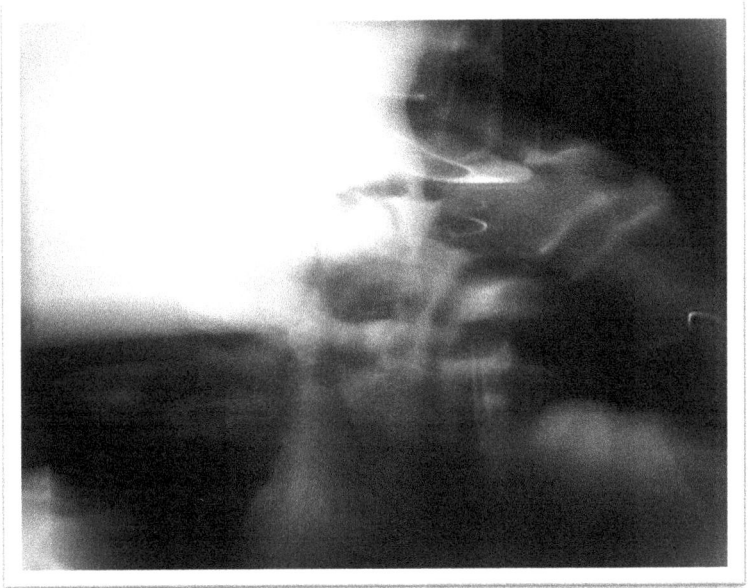

Shake off the dust and put on your glorious garments my
people.

(Isaiah 52.2)

YESHUA

Know Thy Self

To all of us, the common piece of advice is to just be ourselves. The idea is quite appealing, but how many individuals actually have a clue about who they are. Not only do we frequently mix our genuine identity with our ego identity, but we also confuse our dreams, wishes, and limiting beliefs with our true selves. This is not who we are. We have been provided with a very satisfactory response to that inquiry by the spiritual realm. So, who exactly are we, then. As far as we are aware, this is the case. Energy frequencies and vibrations are the only things that exist, according to Einstein and Tesla. Everything else is nothing but energy frequencies and vibrations. Everything is devoid of any kind of solidity. Both you and I are energy fields that have different frequencies and can respond to and interact with other energy fields based on our interactions. We are all like individual vibrations and manifestations, which are also referred to as divine spirit beings of eternal life in the vast ocean known as Yahweh. The scientists believe that the unified field, which is the absolute truth from which we all sprang, is seven-dimensional, and it is impossible for us to comprehend this concept. The power of energy combined with our three-dimensional perspective. As a result, we attribute this energy to a wide variety of names and characteristics in order to better comprehend it. The seven laws of powers of Yahweh, the I am that I am, and the vital force of Yahweh's spirit are all names that we use to refer to this substance. There is no difference between the stream of being of the All-unity awareness or just consciousness; it is all consciousness. A consciousness-seeking experience that takes place through a particular organism is what Deepak Chopra describes as experiencing it. It is the essence of consciousness, which metamorphoses into an unlimited number of shapes and occurrences. Nothing is anything other than consciousness manifesting itself in the shape of form, colour, and sound. This is what creation is, and you and I are individual manifestations that emerge from this stream of consciousness, which is also referred to as light ether or the spirit of Yahweh of the Word of God. We are divine and immortal cosmic beings, and these spheres of light are the undisturbed heavens, which are our homeland, only because we have abused the divine gift of free will are we no longer there. This is the sole reason why we are not there anymore. Because of Lucifer's rebellion, we have gone more and further away from our home, which is the seven-dimensional reality that possesses the highest vibration of love. This has been accomplished by thinking and acting in an increasingly negative manner. Therefore, what occurs to us each time we take on the form of a soul and incarnate into the material universe of time and space, contrasts, and the relationship between cause and effect. When a lovely couple is blessed with the arrival of an infant new baby. It is a fact that the new parents adhere to a particular belief system which is the source of the problem. Every single member of our family, as well as everyone else in their immediate environment, adheres to the same set of beliefs. Every aspect of their belief system was represented by symbols, they adhered to certain clothing standards and belief systems, they carried out activities associated with their belief system, and they venerated that belief. Because we have complete faith in our parents, we almost never question the programming they have given us, and in a short amount of time, we begin to adopt their opinions as our own perspectives. Even in circumstances in which our community instructs us to go out and kill other people who do not believe in their system, we continue to view the world through the same conditioned mindset as our parents do. We carry out their directives with a strong sense of conviction since, in our minds, there is only one belief system, and that is their absolute reality. Think about how many battles have begun in this manner due to the intense cultural connection that exists among us, and the fact that we have never questioned the beliefs that our ancestors had previously. Additionally, we will make certain that our offspring also believe in the order of the world system, and this will ensure that the myth is passed down from one generation to the next. As a group, we have committed ourselves to a completely fictitious and ephemeral identity that has absolutely nothing to do with who we are in our truest form. Would it be possible for false religions to be the only ones that can give us a false identity, which is not true. False identities could also easily be our race or nationality, political affiliation, social or cultural background, body shape, gender, politics, and a great deal of other isolating concepts or teachings that distort our true origin. These are only temporary costumes that our soul wears throughout our brief journey here on planet Earth, and the costumes we wear are determined by the setting in which we were born and the culture into which we were born. Shouldn't Shakespeare have already proclaimed that this earth is nothing more than a stage, and that we are only actors on this stage. If we identify with any of these temporary masks and assume that this is who we truly are, then we have completely lost our divine beginning, which is far beyond the constraints that are imposed by earthly circumstances. Through this compromise, we have given up our heavenly birthright in favour of our ego legacy. The question is, why do we have such a strong desire to identify with this superficiality of the world. A profound sensation of isolation and disconnection is frequently the root cause of our need to be identified and to experience a sense of being unique. Here on Earth, we have the experience of being distinct from deity as well as from one another. The result is that our ego is attached to organisations or communities that have the potential to provide us with a surge of feelings of importance, belonging, and power. When we make an effort to feel superior or exceptional in comparison to other people and start openly flaunting our communal identification, such as our nationality, religion, race, sexual orientation, political affiliation, and so on, this is a strong indication that we might be suffering from profound insecurity. In an effort to persuade people about something that we are obviously still having difficulty with ourselves, we strive to convince them. We do this in the expectation that other people will respect, love, and accept us because, if they do, we will feel validated, and we may also start to respect, love, and accept ourselves. However, this strategy is never successful. Yeshua made the following statement: "Those who do not know themselves want to be confirmed in the world, which results in the creation of after-effects." Once we have become aware of the manipulation that our ego is capable of, we are able to start questioning and investigating everything that we have previously considered to be our identity. It is possible that we will come to the realisation that all we have ever believed in is nothing more than ideas that we have taken from other people and never really questioned. It is quite unlikely that we ever inquire. Is this true in all honesty. What is the truth about who I am. Is this the person I want to be that I am. As soon as we begin to concentrate on our genuine spiritual identity, we start to disassociate ourselves from the values, rituals, traditions, beliefs, and influences that are associated with our origins as well as other cultural, political, and racial groups. We will need to question and let go of anything that ties us to this world and is not in accord with who we truly are in order to go back into a higher frequency that is closer to our true home. Mostly due to the fact that, as I mentioned earlier, our world, our planet Earth, is not our official and permanent residence. In the course of our everlasting journey, our brief stay here, which lasts for fewer than thirty thousand days, is nothing more than a fleeting moment. It is merely an educational environment for the development of our souls. We come to the realisation that we are not defined by our physical body, beliefs, conditioned patterns, ideas, emotions, or even by our personality when we begin to rediscover our genuine essence. This realisation occurs when we begin to rediscover our true essence. When we let go of these world identifications, what is left is our fundamental nature, which is an endless being that exists beyond the confines of time. We were provided with a piece of information that is not only straightforward but also highly effective, and we are able to put it to use. It tells me that although I am a part of this world, I am not of this world. It takes us away from the tiny dramas that we experience on a daily basis and enables us to examine our difficulties as objective spectators. It is the ideal instrument for self-recognition and for making more informed decisions. When we are able to recover our actual identity and remember who we truly are, we become more receptive to receiving divine love, which is our true legacy. From this abundance, we are able to then give love and assistance to other people without expecting anything in return.

The flesh is the learning vessel and is only a temporary
self and we will change in a twinkling of an eye to our true
form. The ego is the belief that the body is the only vessel
you have and is an illusion and not the true you.

(Author)

YESHUA

The Message of the Soul

It is of the utmost significance that we pay attention to our inner voice throughout the day. Our spirit is communicating with us in order to assist us in leading a life that is more optimistic. As we go through our relatively brief existence on earth, let us not forget the reason that the majority of us are here. As a one-of-a-kind opportunity, we have the chance to undo our karma, which is comprised of our misdeeds, and cleanse our spirits. Every unloving experience, emotion, thought, phrase, and action that we have will eventually come back to us. This is what we mean when we talk about karma. In the spiritual realms, the development and purification of our soul can be very slow and difficult. This is due to the fact that we do not have the physical body that can buffer some karmic turmoil, and in addition, we are only surrounded by other souls that are similar to us, and like attracts like. Nevertheless, here on Earth, we do have a physical body that acts as a barrier, and we are exposed to a wide variety of people and points of view that have the potential to challenge and educate us in a more profound manner. Being able to be here at this very moment is therefore a wonderful blessing. Every time we create karma, it is stored in our soul, our body, and most crucially, in the planets that correspond to the repository of that karma to our soul and body. All of this karma will eventually come back to haunt us. It may take the form of trying circumstances, unpleasant individuals, sicknesses, or even the conflict that is brought about by fate. However, they are sending us warning impulses through our souls in order to clear up these karmic burdens before they hit us in full measure. These messages are sent through our souls and then through our nervous systems, which is the link between our souls and our bodies. This occurs before the karmic burdens fully manifest in our lives. In our solar plexus, we frequently experience these sensations, which are characterised by feelings of discomfort. When we first experience anything, we are typically unable to determine if it is a warning, fear, shame, guilt, or something else that occurs suddenly; but, it does cause us to feel restless and uncomfortable. We do not wish to become aware of it or confront it. It is possible for it to be a powerful emotional charge, or it may be a mild charge that we typically ignore as a sensation of boredom or anxiousness. The messages that our soul is sending us and that are rising up in us right now are therefore something that we strive to avoid looking at rather than looking at them instead. Instead, we are currently looking for a stimulant that is more powerful than the message that our soul is trying to convey and that has the ability to override and disregard feelings that are uncomfortable. As an illustration, we might be rushing to the refrigerator or engaging in a variety of other activities that serve as escapes and distractions. Even sex, drink, or narcotics can fall into this category. On the other hand, one of the most common and quickest ways is to lose ourselves in an activity that involves the Internet, our mobile phones, television, binge viewing, or video games. We have come to realise that with just a few clicks, we can be transported to an entirely different universe and reality, and as a result, we no longer experience this unsettling sensation of caution within us. In the event that our chaotic emotional state is too unpleasant, we long for experiences that are incredibly gripping in order to excite us even more and completely numb our feelings. An onslaught of these engrossing and distracting stimulants can be found here on the Internet, on our mobile phones, and on our televisions. These stimulants can be found in exciting news bursts, movies, sports, or computer games. What is it that most likely catches our immediate and full attention. Anything that appeals to our base inclinations, such as violence, greed, power, and sex, is a fundamental component of the most viewed television programmes, the highest grossing movies, the most popular computer games, and even news networks. Do we really believe that a few of hours a day of exposure to things like violence, brutality, murder, torture, dishonesty, porn, and other such content has no impact on us. Consider that if that were the case, all businesses that advertise their wares on television or the internet would be squandering their money. However, these businesses spend billions of dollars because they are certain that they are able to affect us and influence our behaviour through the visual pictures that they present to us. In order to pull us into a lower frequency and dependency, there is a massive industry that serves the objective of intentionally feeding us with false and severe negativity. Because we forget things so rapidly, the human brain has a hard time telling the difference between real and unreal. It is possible that our minds are aware that this is really a movie; nonetheless, our bodies, our brains, and our subconscious all take it as if it were real. The same stress responses are taking place here; they are being responsible for the production of cortisol and adrenaline, as well as the circulation of blood throughout the body. In spite of the fact that the threat may be simulated on a computer screen, or it may actually exist, our glands and hormones will still create the identical chemical reaction. Every one of these dissonances and disharmonies has an effect on the consciousness of our cells and organs, and in particular on our nervous system, which serves as the network that connects our soul to the rest of our body. As a result, tension is created in the delicate vital nerves, which are the conduits through which the life energy runs along the spirit, so ensuring that our body remains healthy and youthful. Are we ever aware of the fact that everything that we go through on a regular basis is kept in our bodies, and naturally, it is also stored in the particles that make up our souls. It has been demonstrated by scientific research that every experience is forever recorded. The truth of this assertion may be attested to by each and every individual who is afflicted with hyperthymia, which is characterised by entire memory recall. No image that we have seen can ever be erased from our memories. Each of us ought to accept complete responsibility for whatever it is that we voluntarily choose to consume. It is common knowledge that if we continue to give our bodies bad food, it will eventually lead to major health issues to be experienced. When it comes to anything that we put into our soul, the same principle applies. Any visual diet consisting of films, games, and shows that do not improve our lives can be detrimental to our souls and, in the end, change who we are and who we are becoming. Is it possible for us to comprehend that when we consciously choose to engage in activities that promote things such as violence, greed, power, and porn, we are lowering our own vibration. When all is said and done, everything in life is vibration. Our immune system is quickly weakened, and as a result, we are more susceptible to a wide variety of infections. Tests have showed that individuals who watched a documentary on Mother Teresa, for example, had a discernible rise in the number of t-cells in their bodies, but individuals who watched a movie showing violence had a significant decrease in the number of t-cells in their bodies. As an additional point of interest, the reduction in our frequency might serve as a gateway or an invitation for bad energy. Following that, they are able to infuse us with Trojan thoughts that have a similar resonance. These are thoughts that we believe to be our own, but they are not. With these Trojan thoughts, they are able to manipulate us for their own nefarious purposes. Furthermore, there is the risk that we will quickly become desensitized and numb to a certain level of violence, brutality, and stimulus, and that we will crave for experiences that are even more intense in order to achieve the same level of satisfaction. There is absolutely nothing wrong with watching movies, shows, games, or sports. In fact, I strongly advocate doing so because these activities can be incredibly enriching to one's life and soul. Our objectives and the reasons we are keeping an eye on them are the things that really count. Do our intents consist of nothing more than a desire to get away from that vexing sensation and message from our soul, which we frequently brush off as being nothing more than anxiety or irritation. There is a very significant message that our soul has for us. In the future, when we experience feelings of boredom or anxiety, let us not try to escape these sensations; rather, let us take a seat, close our eyes, and investigate what these feelings might signify to us. At what point does it bring to mind. Almost anything from our younger years. We are unsure of our own thinking. It is possible that the cause is a false belief. Is there anything that we are attempting to avoid. If yes, let us be completely present with that sensation and allow it to convey to us what it is that our soul desires for us to know. Possibly, we are in for some very pleasant surprises. Even if the lessons that come from our soul are not immediately obvious, there are gifts that are so powerful that we must not disregard them.

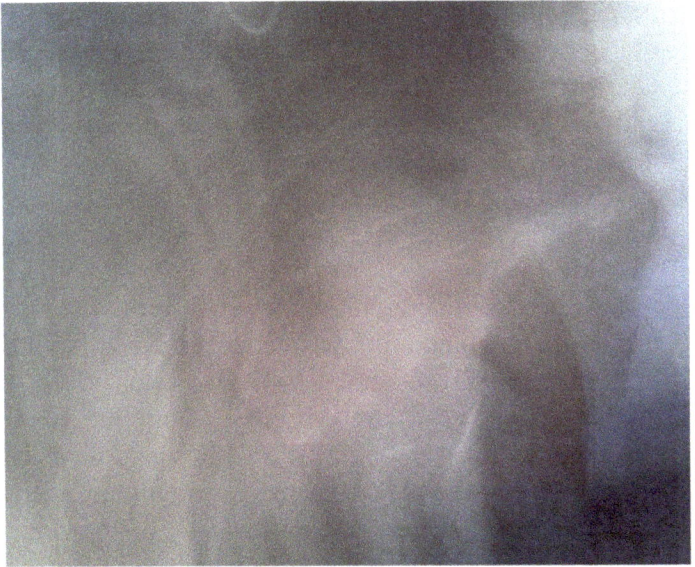

"I am the resurrection and the life. Whoever believes in me, though he dies, yet shall he live, and everyone who lives and believes in me shall never die."

(John 11:25)

YESHUA

Where We Come From

Did you know that there is a story that dates back to ancient times that provides us with definitive answers to the age-old question of all people "Who am I?" My origins are unknown to me. Why am I at this place? so where exactly am I going? Over the course of history, philosophers have developed a multitude of hypotheses that frequently contradict one another. Similarly, the churches have been similarly perplexed and unable to provide satisfactory answers to these concerns ever since they removed the teachings of reincarnation in the sixth century. As a result, the scientific community has endeavoured to fill this void by introducing the concept of evolution. This theory proposes that all of us originated from the ocean and gradually evolved through the animal kingdom to become creatures that resemble humans. Eventually, we arrived at our current "glorious magnificence" of modern man. Depending on the religious beliefs that we hold, we may eventually be able to strum harps around the throne of Yahweh, or we may merge back into some primordial soup, and in due time, we will repeat the same cycle over and over again. However, is that a fact. It has been repeatedly demonstrated to us by prophets and seers that this notion is flawed. This is because the holy realm, which is located in the pure heavens, is a seven-dimensional reality that is our true home. The natural kingdoms did not develop in this particular location on the world. They were only able to adapt to the many habitats that exist on earth. A nourished spiritual atom evolves over aeons of time in rhythmic intervals from the mineral kingdom into the plant kingdom, then into the animal kingdom, and finally into the kingdom of nature beings, with the ultimate goal of becoming a true spirit being, radiant self-luminous divine, and eternal child of Yahweh. True evolution can only take place in the highest spiritual realm, which is the absolute reality. Many people refer to them as angelic beings. Unfortunately, at the` beginning of creation, some of these divine beings, who were the sons and daughters of Yahweh, made the decision to follow a leader who led them away to create a new creation, which was their own creation. They fell from these pure heavens, the absolute reality, into what we call the relative reality of time and space of contrasts, and the law of sowing and reaping brought them down to the three-dimensional material universe, where the planet earth is one of the lowest points in this temporary reality. This was all because they disobeyed the law of love, peace, and harmony. In this most dramatic parable of the "prodigal son," which can be found in Luke 15:11-32, Yeshua communicated not just this process but also the truth about who we are, where we come from, why we are here, and where we are headed. This information was transmitted by Yeshua two thousand years ago. In the beginning of this tale, there was a man who was affluent, possessed property, and employed servants. He also had two sons. To enable him to go out into the world and create his own life and his own reality, the younger one approached his father and requested that he be given his portion of the inheritance. After receiving his portion of the inheritance, the son departs from the residence of his father. Through these remarks, Yeshua provided us with the response to our initial inquiry, which was, "Who are we?" We are all divine spirit beings, just like these sons, and we are the ideal children of Yahweh, who is symbolised here by the wealthy father. In addition, the solution to our following inquiry, which is "where do we come from?" The absolute reality is where we reside in love, serenity, harmony, and the safety that comes from the father. This is our genuine home. To leave this environment of complete wealth was a decision that we made on our own volition. The fact that Yahweh does not interfere with the choices we make is the reason why he allowed us to depart. As a loving father, he gave us our inheritance, which is a piece of energy or life force that allows us to survive. When we departed the absolute reality, this energy potential was bestowed upon each and every one of us. At this point, the narrative continues by informing us that the son went out into the world and squandered his fortune by engaging in unpleasant behaviour. To put it another way, he squandered all of the life force that was bestowed upon him by living a life that was self-centred and selfish, which is the antithesis of love. This is the way that the biblical passage known as "The Fall" describes. It is important to keep in mind that everything, including everything that is absolutely everything, is nothing more than energy, vibrations, and fluctuations. When it comes to vibration, love is the highest vibration here, while matter, which is nothing more than crystallised thought forms, is the lowest vibration. So, the son came from the highest vibration of love and abundance right down to the temporary realm of pain, suffering, and need as explained in the following scripture, "and when he had used up everything meaning the loaned energy, a severe famine came over the country, and he came into want and he moved away and entered the service of a citizen to guard the swine's and he would have been glad to still his hunger with the husks that the pigs ate, but no one gave them to him." Do you not believe that this is what is occurring right now to billions of people all around the world who are homeless, have very little or nothing to eat, and are in a state of profound despair. Our lives here on earth are filled with pain, suffering, and need, which are nothing more than the karmic results of causes that we have made ourselves and

34

are now returning to us. This is true even if we are not personally experiencing such a severe condition. The son has now experienced a profound realization of himself, which also provides a solution to our third question, which is why we are here. "And when he came to his senses, he said how many of my father's servants have bread enough to spare, and I perish with hunger," the story continues. "And how many of them have enough bread to spare?" My father will be the recipient of my visit, and I will tell him, "My father, I have sinned against heaven and before you, and I am no longer worthy to be called your son." I will then set out to go see my father. Please accept me as one of your servants. The son is able to recall his roots, his true home, which was characterised by perfection, luxury, and abundance. Additionally, he acknowledges his errors and, with a great deal of humility, feels profound regret and sorrow for his actions. In the same way that an alcoholic must first descend to the lowest level before he is willing to work himself out of the hole he has created for himself, Christ comes to our aid to assist us in overcoming other karmic burdens through the Christ spark that emanates from our fourth energy centre, also known as the chakra. This spark assists us in transforming our karma, thereby transforming the negative energy into positive energy. Repentance, forgiveness, making amends, and refraining from violating the Law of Love are the means by which we can improve our current low energy vibration and bring it back into alignment with the highest love vibration. We have come to this place in order to regain our divine and pure nature, just as we were before we abandoned the absolute reality that existed before the fall. Because of this, everything that we come across in our lives here on earth is specifically designed to return us back to our origins. When the father saw his son, he was filled with sympathy for him. He raced to his son, threw his arms around him, and kissed him. Now, what occurs next in the story is that the young man was still a long way off. Because of this incredible portrayal, we can understand why some people refer to this as "The story of the running father." It has been said that if we take one step towards Yahweh, he will take a thousand steps towards us. This is something that we have all heard. This demonstrates the amazing love that Yahweh, the father, has for us, as well as his tremendous desire for us to come back to him and be with him. The continuing portion of the story is as follows: "The son told his father, I have sinned against heaven and against you." At this point, I am no longer deserving of the title of your son. However, the father gave orders to his staff to fetch the best robe as quickly as possible, to put a ring on his finger, to put shoes on his feet and to make arrangements for a feast to rejoice because "this son of mine was dead and is alive again, he was lost and is found, so they began to celebrate." The fact that Yahweh, our father, does not consider the inadequacies and crimes of his children is something that Christ brings to our attention. Instead, he is only concerned with what he has made, which is pure, noble, and good. After then, the narrative continues with the second son being rather displeased with the lavish feast and welcome that was given to his brother. On the other hand, the father reminds him, "My son, you are always with me, and everything that I have possesses you." The fact that your brother was dead and is now alive again, that he was lost and is now discovered, and that we should be happy and delighted at this time is nonetheless appropriate. The fact that we are all heirs to infinity is brought to our attention since we are all sons and daughters of divinity. And those spirit beings who have never left the seven-dimensional pure reality have always been able to experience complete and utter peace, harmony, love, and abundance. Every time I tell this story, it makes my heart feel a little bit better because I know, on some level, that this story provides answers to all four questions that I have regarding my existence.

The Kingdom of Yahweh is in you and all around you and
is not in the things created by man.

(Nag Hammadi)

YESHUA

Free Will

If someone believes that our free will is nothing more than a hormonal impulse in our brain, then they do not comprehend the capabilities of this potent instrument, the reasons why we possess it, or the ways in which we may use our free will to alter every aspect of our lives. To enable us to be cocreators, to love and serve without self-interest, and to participate in Yahweh's magnificent infinite creation of the absolute reality that is in a state of exponential, perpetual motion, continual expansion, and evolution, Yahweh bestowed upon each and every one of us, as His children, the gift of two distinct qualities: eternal life and our own personal free will. This heavenly gift of free will has unfortunately been misappropriated by certain celestial spiritual beings for the purpose of achieving their own self-centred aims and has been transformed into their ego will. Over the course of time, they have, among other things, established the reality of time and space, contrasts, light and shadow, good and evil, and, most crucially, the law of cause and effect. They have also established the truth of the temporary and relative reality. Because of the rule of sowing and reaping, these spiritual beings that have fallen into a state of disrepair are able to experience and understand the repercussions of their acts anytime they have chosen to abuse their free will. The purpose of this is not to punish but rather to educate. They would produce causes that are stored as soul burdens in the planets, and from there, they would eventually come back to them as karma. This would happen each time they performed an action that was contrary to the law of love. There is a possibility that these karmic impacts will occur within the same lifetime or thousands of lifetimes later. However, the mercy of Yahweh enables us to get free of our karmic or soul weights at any time by repenting, forgiving, asking for forgiveness, making reparations, and refraining from doing the things that we have done wrong. To our great regret, the vast majority of people are unaware of the fact that everything that occurs to us is the consequence of a cause that we have initiated in the past. There is no such thing as an accident; this is the application of the law of cause and effect. The conclusion is that a higher force, such as Yahweh, does not determine our destinies or our fates for us. Always, it is decided and constructed by the decisions that we have made in the past. And yet, when something happens to us, such as a crisis, a blow from fate, a bad relationship, and so on, we rarely investigate the reasons why this is happening to us. Instead of responding, we simply react, which frequently involves blaming others, blaming Yahweh, blaming circumstances, and looking for vengeance and punishment, which ultimately results in more trouble. Therefore, is there any other way to put an end to this insanity. Truly repenting and forgiving are the true components to healing the division. You will achieve more in this world through acts of mercy than you will through acts of retribution. The strategy is to stop any further negative development occurring. A portion of the explanation can be found in the famous words of Albert Einstein, which state that "Problems cannot be solved by the same level of thinking that were responsible for creating them." When the United States of America retaliated, it did so by using the same level of ruthless force and weapons that the terrorists had used. Confronting the atrocities committed by war with a higher level of consciousness, which should be transformed into the capacity of forgiveness to aid in the healing process. In the event that we are confronted with a crisis, difficulties, challenging persons, or circumstances, the following are three significant ways in which we might make use of our free will. Our first option is to respond. The initial emotional impulse that we experience is typically what sets off our reactions. Benjamin Rebid examined this quick reaction and discovered that our brain already knows our decision milliseconds before we are consciously aware of it. This discovery was made by Benjamin Rebid. We are not truly exercising our free will when we merely react by following the emotional and hormonal impulses that we are experiencing. On the contrary, we are largely governed by the programmed programming that we have received from our parents, instructors, or early life experiences. This conditioning encompasses our goals, beliefs, and temperaments. All of our responses originate from the level of our ego, which frequently asserts that it is the victim and demands retribution and punishment. This merely results in additional karma, as we have seen in the case of the United States of America. Using our own free will to respond is the second option available to us. Keep in mind the time-honoured piece of advice: before you speak or act, count to ten. To respond is to say that. In this situation, it is not our ego that has the opportunity to step in; rather, it is our higher self, our authentic self. Every time you respond, you are engaging in a moment of introspection. When we do this, it indicates that we take the new problem seriously and recognise that nothing occurs by chance. Now is the time for self-awareness to take place. Through the process of making conscious decisions in the here and now, we are able to discover our own way out of this conflict, clear up what we can, forgive, and move on with our lives. In most cases, a reaction is a solution that will address the well-being and unity of all parties involved, and the following is the third possibility, by exercising our free will, we are able to alter our mindset. It is possible that we are unable to alter the reality around us; but we always have the ability to alter our perspective on the world or on any particular challenge that we are confronted with. This indicates that we search for the hidden treasure that may be in a challenging situation. This is due to the fact that nothing can exist without the power of Yahweh, which is the positive aspect throughout everything. When it comes to you, there is no such thing as a problem that does not hold a gift in its possess. In order to acquire their gifts, you actively seek out troubles. From a strict standpoint, everything is medicine; everything is here to heal us and to bring us home. This is due to the fact that there is a throbbing divine love in everything, even in the unfortunate circumstances. Also, the majority of our old views are a result of previous life experiences and the conditions that were imprinted into us by other people. To avoid getting caught up and trapped by attitudes that are harmful to ourselves and others, it is most important on the spiritual path to become conscious of and familiar with our previous attitudes about everything. This is done so that we do not get caught up in attitudes that are harmful to ourselves and others. We have the ability to change things by altering our attitude, which will allow us to appreciate the half full glass rather than ignoring the half empty glass. When we questioned them, we change them. We can choose to view a crisis as a stepping stone rather than a stumbling stone since it has the potential to provide us with opportunities for growth. We have the ability to turn the lemon into lemonade if we adopt a different mentality. As time goes on, we come to realise that everything can be found in this world for our benefit. Acceptance and moving on are both facilitated by this. There is a possibility that we will even come to appreciate the circumstance, given that nothing happens to us but just for us. With our free will, we're making hundreds of decisions every day, and these choices operate like a chisel that gradually sculpts our character and yes, in the end, even our physical appearance. When we are young, our faces appear clear and smooth;

nevertheless, the decisions we make in life will affect how we will look when we are older. If we have made decisions that are mostly self-centred and selfish, if we have blamed the world for everything, and if we have become resentful and difficult, then this will be evident. On the other hand, if our decisions have been made with love, gentleness, kindness, and selflessness in mind, then that will also be evident. We can either appear more pleasant or more sour. We need to take a look at ourselves in the mirror, but we also need to know how we have exercised our free will up to this point. As divine spiritual beings, we were endowed with the ability to exercise free will and endless existence. It is possible for us to hasten our return to our true home, the absolute reality, so that we might once again be divine co-creators of creation. This can be accomplished by aligning our free will with Yahweh's divine will of love and unity, which is the appropriate application of our free will from moment to moment.

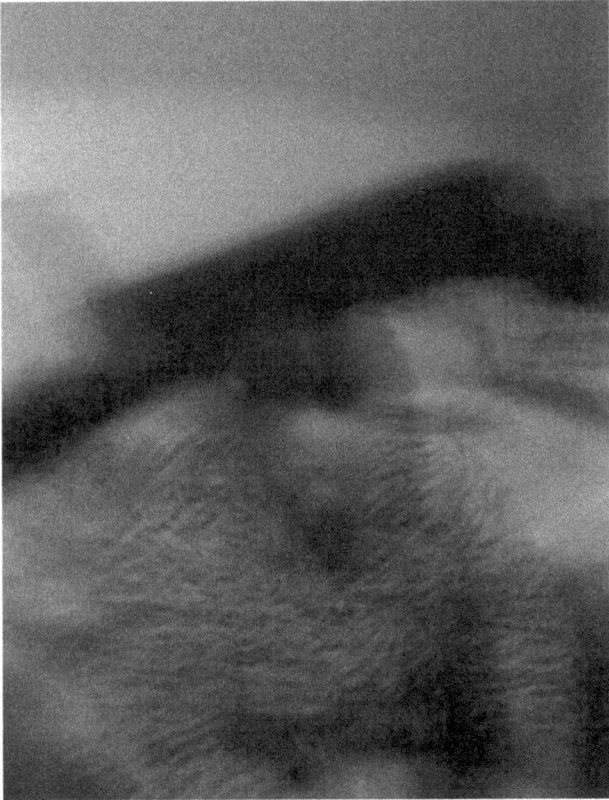

Jesus said, "If the flesh came into being because of spirit, it is a marvel, but if spirit came into being because of the body, it is a marvel of marvels. "Yet I marvel at how this great wealth has come to dwell in this poverty."

(Gospel of Thomas)

43

YESHUA

Reflection

The Law of Reflection is a component of the Law of Sowing and Reaping, as well as a component of the Law of Karma, which governs the causal chain of events. Because of this law, both our perceptions of the world around us and the world's perceptions of us are determined. Consciousness, which is energy that fluctuates in a wide variety of vibrational frequencies, is the primary component of everything that exists. It is always possible for the greatest, most pure, and most noble vibration or frequency to penetrate the lower vibration, which includes matter, which is also nothing more than changed down energy and vibration of the lowest quality. It is impossible for the lower to permeate the higher. The fact that any high vibration that is able to pierce another high vibration does not produce any shadow or reflection is something that we are aware of, of course. Due to the fact that everything permeates everything else, there are no shadows in the pure heavens, which is the absolute reality. The situation is totally different for us people who live on this planet. Because of our frequency, we are unable to pierce matter. Therefore, we only project our thinking and our acts onto the surface of whatever surrounds us, and matter only reflects back to us that what we have sent out, our thinking and our deeds. We are merely experiencing our own projections, which are reflected or mirrored back to us once we have experienced them. What we are experiencing right now is our life, our reality, and it is just like that. Currently, we are experiencing that condition of consciousness. When we gaze at a lake with our human eyes, we can only see the reflection on the surface. However, creatures with higher vibrations are able to see through everything, including the surface of the lake, and perceive the abundant life that is vibrating below. According to Yahweh, the depth of the lake represents life. The distinction between high vibrational penetration and low vibrational reflection in our relative and temporary reality of time and space is that the former is more intense than the latter. We are similar to a caterpillar that is encased in a cocoon. The cocoon represents our own self-made ego-world, which is comprised of all of our bad feelings, ideas, words, and actions during our lifetime. Every single one of our programmes. The entirety of all that is not yet in accordance with the divine law of love that is unselfish. These aspects of human nature that have not been resolved manifest themselves as pictures that are a part of the walls of our cocoon, and that is what we are always staring at. This is because these walls are like mirrors, reflecting back to us who we still are and what we have sent out into the world. This is the only way that we can see ourselves. The rule of reflection makes this statement. It is fascinating to take into consideration that the human eye does not actually see reality. It is only able to register what we, as humans, have projected, which includes our programmes, our karmic responsibilities, our beliefs, our anxieties, our habits, and so on. They are the walls that are the radiation of our aura, the plasma or corona, and that is also something that we are aware of and can discuss. As far as we are able to comprehend, that is all. Nothing else is known to us. Everyone is living in their own aura, the cocoon that they have constructed for themselves with their own set of beliefs and programmes. Currently, we are experiencing that condition of consciousness. In general, we might be able to reach a consensus on terminology such as red, black, white, meadow, woodland, house, moon, and stars from a collective standpoint. Nevertheless, the way in which we experience these things is entirely dependent on the personal programmes and beliefs that we have, which are the components that comprise our cocoon and through which we view the world as if through a pair of glasses. The way you perceive the world is how it actually is. Some viewers, for instance, will get a sense of dread when they look at the picture of the nuclear vessel. In some people, it will be the opposite, a sense of power and strength that they experience. It is entirely dependent on the person who is looking at it as to how it is interpreted. It is important to pay attention to the first concept or association that comes to mind when you view a picture of an apple, as well as the feeling that the picture evokes in you. What do you see as a sign of health that prevents you from going to the doctor? or a fruit that has been genetically modified and intensively sprayed? going for a stroll through an apple orchard? Do you have fond recollections of grandma's apple pie? Apple computers, tales such as Adam and Eve, Snow White, William Tell, and many of the Greek mythologies that are all about an apple or something very personal, and so on and so forth. In what ways does it cause you to reflect back. When viewed through the lenses of our aura, the apple seems to us. The same personal memories, beliefs, judgements, prejudices, and programmes that we have formed are being reflected back to us by it. On because of this, each individual perceives the apple in a unique manner and responds to it in a unique manner. The fact that this is not a new finding is obvious. According to the ancient teachings of the Talmud, "we do not see things as they are, we see them as we are." This message has been passed down to us. Absolutely everything that surrounds us is nothing more than a mirror of who we are. I will provide you with one more illustration in case you are still unsure. In the following experiment, the psychiatrist Oscar Janiger was the one who carried it out. An artist was given doses of

250 micrograms of LSD that were separated by an hour, and they were asked to draw multiple sketches of the physician who provided the medication over the course of eight hours. Throughout the course of the eight hours, a variety of sketches were created of the physician. It is obvious that the Doctor Who did not change his appearance; rather, the artist's altered state of awareness and his cocoon or aura were the factors that brought about the shift. Have we come to the realisation that the way we perceive the environment around us is always determined by the thoughts that are going through our heads. No matter what happens, the movie that we watch on the outside is always playing in our heads; it is never the other way around. It is only because the outer world reflects back to us what is already present within us that it can cause us to feel disturbed in any way. The rule of reflection makes this statement. Due to the fact that no two states of awareness are identical, each of us has a very unique perspective on the world. It is true that every single person lives in their very own cocoon, their very own bubble, and their very own personal echo chamber. Exactly the same as in a snow globe. Every single individual in our immediate vicinity is wrapped up in their own private snow globe, and they only see themselves. Another way to think about it is that they exist in their very own universe. To put it another way, this planet is home to roughly eight billion parallel worlds, and each individual perceives himself to be the ultimate centre of his or her own universe. However, the key to our freedom is also concealed within our own particular cocoon or universe. There are no mishaps that occur in lifetime. Not a single thing occurs by chance. This also encompasses what we see, or the things that our eyes choose to focus on from one moment to the next. What or someone garners our attention is the question. More specifically, when the things that we see cause us to experience an emotional response and strike a chord with us. I am referring to the law of resonance. If we did so, we

would learn something. There is a special message for us. What is it that we need to make clear and for which we also need to accept responsibility. This is what Carl Jung had to say about it: "Everything that irritates us about other people can lead us to an understanding of ourselves." Getting to know ourselves better is the first step on the road to achieving perfection.

The Saviour swallowed up death - (of this) you are not reckoned as being ignorant - for he put aside the world which is perishing. He transformed himself into an imperishable aeon and raised himself up, having swallowed the visible by the invisible, and he gave us the way of our immortality.

(Nag Hammadi)

YESHUA

Life After Death

The spiritual world has provided us with some extremely useful and intriguing suggestions that the majority of people are not aware of. Our journey into the spiritual realms, which many people refer to as death, has provided us with these suggestions. Taking cremation as an example, we may question oneself if we would rather be buried or cremated. These days, over sixty percent of people in the United States opt for cremation rather than burial. When compared to graves, it does have certain advantages in terms of economics, hygiene, and protecting the environment. When it comes to cremation and burial, the majority of religions have various laws. It is customary for traditional Jews to bury the deceased within twenty-four hours, with a few notable exceptions. The only thing that traditional Muslims believe in is burial. A significant portion of the Christian community has been opposed to cremation because of a biblical passage that discusses the resurrection of the physical body on the day of judgement. against the other hand, the Catholic Church has done away with its prohibition against cremation since 1963. It is possible that it would be beneficial for us to first examine what actually occurs at the time of death in order to make the best decisions for ourselves and for other people. Let us begin with a person who has, for the most part, lived their life in accordance with the spiritual rules of love and who does not have any fear of death because he is aware that life is eternal and will continue in the spiritual world after his material existence has come to an end. In the process of the soul's unfolding from the physical body, the silver cord, the connection to the body is severed. For each and every one of us, that is the moment of death. In the case of a soul that has been adequately prepared, there are no longer any energetic links or attachments present to its mortal shell. After that, the soul takes a position next to its deceased body and continues to breathe in a completely new rhythm. This occurs based on the manner in which the soul passed away. It is in your best interest to keep in mind that the soul is now capable of not only hearing every word that is spoken in the vicinity, but also sensing all of the thoughts and feelings of people in the room and throughout the world. Now, the soul receives assistance from spiritual entities such as its guardian angel and the souls of previous friends and relatives who have reached a higher level of development. They extend a warm welcome to the soul that is distancing itself from matter and assist it in locating its place in the afterlife. In the eyes of such a soul, death is nothing more than the completion of their education on Earth. There is an occasion going on. When one makes this shift from the material world into the spiritual realms, it is the perfect transfer. In this kind of situation, it is not important whether the body is cremated or buried after at least two or three days have passed because there are some souls that require a little bit more time to completely disengage from the body. When a loved one passes away, unfortunately, people do not give this much attention to the situation, and they frequently have the impression that they need to move quickly in order to get the body out of the way now that the individual has passed away. As an additional option, they might decide to make the arrangements for the funeral at a funeral home or a church ceremony, both of which can be quite solemn instances. Because it is quite likely that the soul will be present during the ceremony, we must ask ourselves whether or not the person who is passing away truly desires to witness and experience the tears and sorrow that occur at such events. Would it be their wish to be mourned. Christ warned us, "Do not mourn your dead, for the one who mourns the loss of a person does not consider the gain of the soul which, if it has lived in me, the Christ enters into higher consciousness spheres of life." This is a reminder that we should not be saddened by the death of individuals. But the situation is very different when the individual did not make preparations for death, if he lived solely on the material level, without any spiritual aspirations, and without being oriented to the divine. In this case, his thinking and striving, as well as his entire consciousness, are strongly fixed on the living conditions of the human life on earth, which he desperately clings to. The soul of such a person is extremely attached to the physical body since it is the only identity and life that the soul is familiar with and believes in. When the time comes for the soul to pass away, it opposes the letting go of the body, which might cause the cutting of the silver cord to be delayed. Because there are no longer any brain waves, a person in this situation would be considered to be terminally ill from a medical point of view. In point of fact, however, it is possible that this soul is still very much connected to the body by the silver cord. Everything that is happening to the body at this moment is still being felt very strongly by the soul. For instance, organ transplants are performed on patients who have been deemed to be brain dead but whose hearts continue to beat and whose bodies continue to breathe. The soul is able to fully sense and experience the process of the body being torn apart and organs being removed from it. This is the reason why the body needs to be sedated before the transplant in order to prevent the well-known "Lazarus effect" or other violent responses by the organ donor. These reflexes are brought on by the severe pain that the soul goes through because of the donation. An individual who has been medically determined to be brain dead does not typically have his or her soul removed from his or her body, which continues to breathe and has a heartbeat. The so-called corpse that is going to be cremated or buried will go through something that is comparable to the removal of organs if the information cord, which is also a conductor of pain and connects the soul and the body, is not completely removed from the person who is dying. When it comes to this particular individual, it can take several days or perhaps longer before the silver court is completely severed. It is very dependent on the manner in which the individual lived during the time period in question. It is helpful to keep in mind that passing away is a process. Because of this, many different cultures have the tradition of holding a wake, which might last for several days for a variety of reasons. However, even if the silver thread is entirely severed, the consciousness of a soul that is not yet fully matured spiritually can still cling to the deceased physical body. Rather than through the silver cable, using magnetic currents or threads is the method. These magnetic currents, the connection to the body, and the physical house of the individual are stronger when the individual's thoughts and interests are focused on the earthly existence and the enjoyment of material pleasures. This is because the individual believes that life can only be experienced in a material body. Should we now be able to recognise that burial, particularly embalming or mummification, can result in such souls clinging to their cherished but deteriorating corpse for decades, if not centuries? In the same way, religious ideas might bring about this effect. For example, the concept that on the day of judgement, their buried bones will be revived anew has kept countless souls who have been brainwashed with religious beliefs linked to their graves for hundreds of years. Let's also talk about the many souls that are unaware that they have passed away, particularly in cases of unexpected death such as accidents or when the individual simply does not believe in the existence of life after death. They are prone to experiencing disorientation and confusion. In addition to causing harm to themselves and others, they have the potential to become what we refer to as earthbound spirits. On our planet, there are millions of them wandering around among us individuals. According to Christ, "The opinion of the human being forms the bond which, after the passing of the body, draws the soul back to where it once enjoyed its passions and pleasures as a human being." This is a reminder that we should constantly keep in mind. In the event that you continue to be an alcoholic until the very end of your existence on earth, your soul will then be reunited with other alcoholics. When there is an excess of food and stimulants, the soul of a glutton will feel as though they have arrived at their home. When people concentrate their primary attention on pleasures and other similar activities, it will be pulled to those areas. When a person is addicted to drugs, their soul will once again be located in the same place where they live and where they can access these substances. The individual who gives in to their desires and passions will, as a soul, discover that they are among individuals who think and live in a similar manner. One more possibility is that a soul that does not have any inklings about the spiritual life and does not know where they are going upon death can get caught up in the darkness and push themselves back into another incarnation instead of moving forward. Can we now understand how important it is for us to know as much as possible about the spiritual aspects of life. This is because there is a possibility that a soul that does not know where they are going after death gets caught up in the darkness. It is a well-known fact in the spiritual realm that the manner in which a person passes away is contingent upon the beliefs and circumstances of that individual.

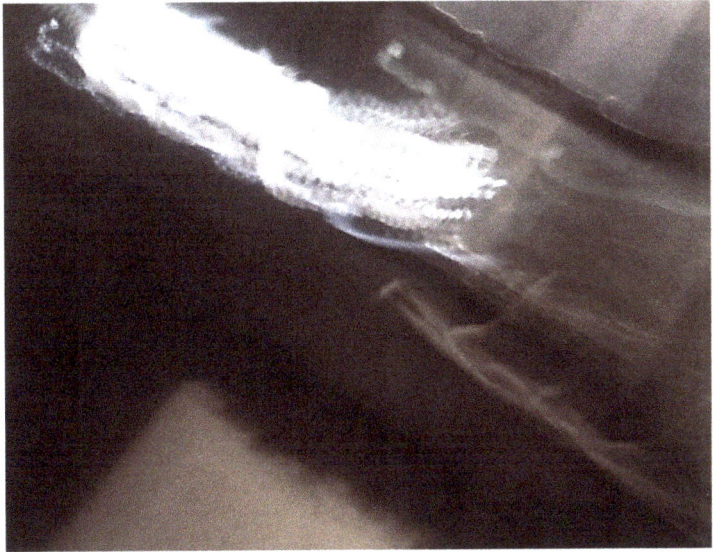

Therefore, when the womb of the soul, by the father's will, turns itself inward, she is baptized and immediately cleansed of external pollution forced upon her, just as dirty clothing is soaked in water and stirred until the dirt is removed and it is clean. So, the cleansing of the soul is to recover the freshness of her former nature and to become as she was.

(Nag Hammadi)

YESHUA

Death and Dying

To begin, I would like to discuss the spiritual aspects that are associated with death and dying. At this point, you might be thinking that speaking about mortality is a depressing topic to discuss. In our culture, we will do anything to prevent people from thinking about death and dying, but the reason for this is that the majority of people are unaware of what is truly taking place at that same moment, and we are always afraid of things that we do not know much about. Death is honoured in many different cultures because it is seen as the deliverance of the soul from the toil and hardship of earthly existence. For example, the early Christians celebrated this moment of transition with a sense of reverence. They had the knowledge that the soul is eternal and that it is now making its way back to the spiritual world. Additionally, they were aware that excessive mourning and grief would only slow down the soul's journey back to its previous location. According to the spiritual law of love, death can be a very beneficial and even beautiful event for anyone who has lived their life according to this principle. In their eyes, it is the same as the day they receive their diploma from their Planetary Education. Now, let's take a look at what happens at the precise instant that a person passes away. In its most basic form, death can be defined as the disconnection of the soul from its physical body. This form of separation might take place gradually over the course of years or all of a sudden for example, as a result of an accident or a heart attack. It is essential to be aware that everyone passes away at precisely the right moment. There is no room for error in the event that a person passes away within six days, six months, or sixty years, regardless of whether the cause of death is an accident or natural causes. This entire process is meticulously planned out by the soul before it takes on a physical form. It is important to keep in mind that earthly existence is not the end destination for the soul. The place of learning is little more than an educational establishment or school, and some students graduate earlier than others. What matters is the lessons that the soul desires to learn and the experiences that it desires to have. However, what occurs from this point on throughout the actual process of dying. As it takes its final breath, the spirit separates itself from the body and continues to breathe in a rhythm that is completely different from what it was before. It is possible for this procedure to take seconds, hours, or even days. Certain souls have difficulty releasing their attachment to the body. Even in the event that it is no longer possible to measure the brain waves, it is still possible for the soul to be connected to the body through the information cord, which is also referred to as the silver cord in the Bible. It is this cord that serves as the connection between the soul and the body, and it is especially important during the dream stage when we are either leaving our body or the soul is leaving the body. This information cord, also known as the silver cord, is always connected to it, and as soon as we wake up, it rapidly brings the soul back into the body. The significance of this cannot be overstated, especially for souls that have passed away in a manner that was sudden and unexpected, or for souls that are unable to come to terms with the truth that they are not truly dead as they had anticipated. As a result of their confusion, they may not want to let go of their physical body, which is the only identity they are familiar with, and they may cling to this lifeless body. They have recently learned that they are still alive, but they are unsure of where to go or what to do next. When the medical team discovers that a person is a flat liner, let's take the time to examine this one thing, especially for anyone who is contemplating donating their organs at that same moment. This indicates that there is no longer any activity in the brain. They pull the physical body apart and remove all of the organs that they deem necessary for their purposes. If the soul is no longer connected to the body, then this is acceptable; however, if it is still connected, then the soul will experience the tremendous anguish that is associated with such a cruel procedure. Completely and utterly. In certain instances, the soul may even be bound to the person who receives its organ for a considerable amount of time in the future. Until the silver cord has been completely severed, the soul will not have completely separated itself from the body until that time has passed. When this occurs, there is no connection between the soul and its mortal shell, and for a period of time, the soul may remain in close proximity to its physical body. For a great number of years, that has been its mode of transportation. It is important to keep in mind that at this level, the soul is also able to hear every word that is uttered and perceive every idea that is being thought by persons who are present in the room. It is possible that souls that have lived intelligently and have not squandered their time on earth will not feel a bridge of light forming for them, even though they may have the desire to cross it. This light is becoming progressively more powerful and brighter towards the other end of the spectrum. It is a radiation of the Guardian being that escorted the soul until it returned to the light, and it continues to do so at this time. It is possible that the soul will be greeted by some of its family or friends who had passed away in the past, and the experience will be similar to that of waking up from a dream. In comparison to the world they had left behind on earth, the new environment seems to be far more genuine. This is how it typically is, and it is just stunning; there is no reason to be terrified of these things. Both you and I have done it a great number of times in the past. The process by which living spirits who are nearing the end of their lives struggle to let go of their worldly existence. There are some souls that, after their spiritual death, have a strong attachment to their earthly life and the identity they achieved on earth. That can be connected to a particular relationship, fortune, prestige, property, or addictions, and they will have a tough time letting go of all that they have valued so highly. Souls who are identified with these things can become what is commonly referred to as earthbound since they are rooted to the earth. In spite of the fact that they may not even acknowledge that they have passed away, they may continue to believe that they are still alive and attempting to carry on with their lives as they did before they went to their places of employment. They make an effort to communicate with any and all people in their immediate vicinity when they are residing in their own homes. It is unfortunate for them that nobody sees or acknowledges them because they are operating on a different vibration than everyone else. They are able to remain in this position for a considerable amount of time until they eventually get so lonely, bored, exhausted, and unhappy. It is possible that they will eventually come to terms with the truth that they have passed on, at which point they will be prepared to receive direction from their spiritual being in order to assist them in returning home once and for all. There are two amazing films that do an excellent job of depicting this occurrence. The first of these films is called The Sixth Sense, and it stars Bruce Willis. The second movie is called The Others, and it stars Nicole Kidman. Both of these shows are worth watching because they provide a genuine illustration of the life of a soul that is rooted on Earth. But there is another reason why we cling, or why certain souls should hold to their life here on earth, and that is because they don't want to face their life pictures or their souls' images right now. This is the reason why we cling. Everything that has been done, thought about, spoken, and done is included here. Those things that have been stored in our soul garment and in the depository planets, and shortly after death, everything that we have done to other people and to ourselves is displayed to us in pictures of what is better known as in the movie. It is a review of our lives; our entire lives pass by more quickly than a movie in a matter of minutes. During this life review, we will experience how our ideas, words, and deeds had affected other people, and we will profoundly feel what they had felt. This is because we are fully awake, and we are evaluating our previous earthly life down to its most trivial sense. As a result, this may serve as a wake-up call for a good number of us. In most cases, we review our life in the presence of our spiritual guide, and in some cases, with the assistance of a spirit guide or guides. The sole criterion that we use to evaluate our life is whether or not we have accomplished the objective of that life and the realisation of unconditional love. Instead of being a judgment of the Creator, we will be the judge of our own lives. However, because we are aware of who we typically are, we will be the harshest judges of both ourselves and others. It goes without saying that this can be a very terrifying experience for somebody who has only ever lived on the material plane, without any intentions of going to a spiritual level. As a result of the fact that the solidity is unable of imagining a life apart from the material existence, he fights against death throughout his existence. Once this soul has been detached from the body and is no longer attached to the earth, it moves in accordance with the principle of spiritual gravity. Moreover, the law asserts that like attracts like. It will go and continue its road with it back to the divine in the spiritual realm that corresponds to the vibration of the soul; however, if the soul has mistreated itself during the previous incarnation on Earth, it may actually find itself in a lower level than it was in the previous existence. In addition to the films "The Sixth Sense" and "others," I would also recommend films such as "Astral City," "Ghost," and "Flatliners." All of them are demonstrating a variety of spiritual truths regarding the processes involved in death.

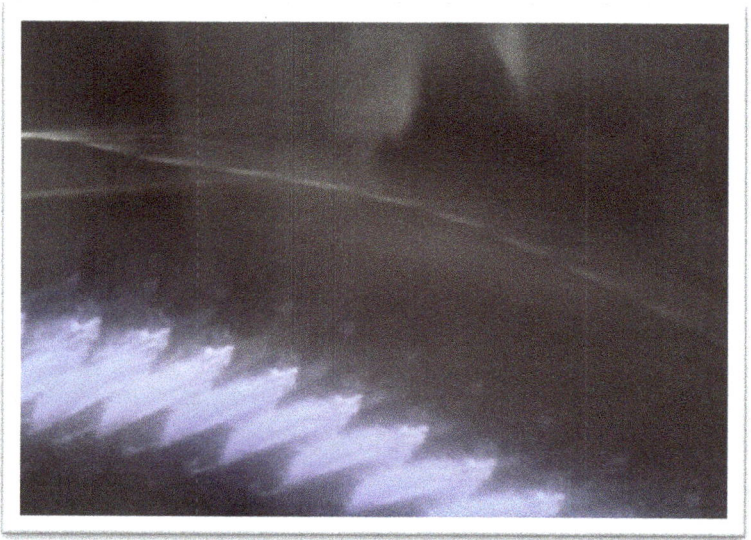

When you know yourselves, then you will be known, and
you will understand that you are children of the living
father. But if you do not know yourselves, then you dwell
in poverty, and you are poverty.

(Gospel of Thomas)

YESHUA

Yeshua Taught Reincarnation

Karma, naturally, refers to the concept of flesh, and incarnation refers to the process by which a soul or spirit enters a physical human body. Reincarnation, on the other hand, refers to the recurrent return of that soul or spirit into a human body. We are spiritual beings by nature, which are also referred to as souls; the genuine fact of our existence is, of course, an aspect of spirit. What is the reason that some of us would wish to incarnate, which means to enter the physical body that we have here on Earth. The reasons are numerous and varied. There are those who come here to observe, those who come here to help other souls, those who come to investigate, and those who simply come to enjoy the physicality of this place. Reincarnation provides us with the opportunity to finish and heal anything that has not been resolved or completed in a previous lifetime, and as souls, we intuitively know that this is something that we need to do. However, the vast majority of us come here because we are bound to the cycle of reincarnation, which means that we still have unfinished business here on earth. Because of what we still need to clean up, as well as any hurt, pain, or loss that has not been atoned for or forgiven, we will be called back into another life. Therefore, we have a strong desire to make apologies or feel the effects that others once endured as a result of our ideas, words, and deeds, which is referred to as karma. Although nobody is forcing us to leave, we are aware that we will not be able to make any spiritual progress until we have healed everything that is located down here. Therefore, we make the decision to reincarnate once more out of our own free will each and every time. Our future family members on earth are the souls with whom we frequently share the most of our karma. They are the members of our future family. Not only that, but they have arrived here for the same reason with each other and with us, in order to heal and prevail over the karmas of the past. Because of this, they are typically of a frequency that is comparable to our own, which is significant since we are aware that our soul can only be attracted to parents who experience vibrations that are comparable to our own. There is a possibility that we have been members of this particular family on numerous occasions in the past, but in various constellations and possibly in different sects. There is a possibility that we have been the mother or father of our future parents in a previous life. As a family, we have created causes that are now affecting us collectively as a result of karma. Now that we have the opportunity to reincarnate again, we can break these chains and undo this, which will ultimately lead to freedom for both of us. All of the other people that we come into contact within our lives, whether it be at work, in groups, or in our neighbourhoods, are affected by the events that take place here and inside this family. When we find ourselves drawn to or repulsed by certain individuals, it is typically an indication that there are some karmic links that need to be resolved. At this point, you might be wondering whether or not all of this is true, and why we don't know much about reincarnation or karma. In any case, it is not absolutely necessary to have knowledge of reincarnation in order to have a successful existence here on earth. Each one of us is provided with a set of beautiful tools that instruct us on how to conduct our lives here on earth. A significant number of souls incarnate into societies that have a single authoritative book of wisdom. That can be the Torah, the Bible, the Koran, and so on; in all of them, they contain the same fundamental laws of life, including the golden rule, which states that you should not do to other people what you would not want them to do to you. Despite the fact that they use different language to express it, the concept is the same. In addition, the western world has the Ten Commandments and the Sermon on the Mount among its other religious texts. They are uncomplicated, highly straightforward, and not difficult in any way. In a few words, we are guided to refrain from killing, lying, cheating, stealing, having idols, respecting our parents, and helping and assisting those who are less fortunate than we are. We are also instructed to avoid having idols. Above all else, however, to love and honour Yahweh, who is present in each and every one of us and in everything that surrounds us. The issue is that we are aware of all of these fundamental guidelines for living before our incarnation; nevertheless, once we are here on this earthly plane, we have a tendency to forget that we are surrounded by a great deal of distractions and temptations. namely, that we have a tendency to lose our values and the reason that we came into existence. When we allow ourselves to become engulfed by our ego, materialism, and selfishness, we run the risk of making a mistake that is either fresh or similar to one we have made in the past. As a result, we become even more ensnared in the cycle of reincarnation. However, if we spend our lives in a mindful manner, adhering to the fundamental principles of life such as the Golden Rule and the ten commandments, we have the ability to raise the vibration of our spirit. When we pass away, our souls will be drawn to a greater state of existence than we were before we incarnated. This means that when we die, our souls will be attracted to us. In the end, we will no longer require this cycle of life and death here on earth, and we will be able to continue with our learning and our development of consciousness in the higher realms from that point on. Right now, some of us might be wondering why we often don't remember any of the lives we've lived in the past. Because we are supposed to live in the here and now, and because having precise knowledge about our previous incarnations would only be a burden for us, this information is purposefully concealed from us. Give it some thought. It's possible that we did it. Maybe we have created hundreds of lives in the past, and many of them have been filled with terrible things that we have done. This information, on its own, would cast a shadow over the choices we make when carrying out our everyday responsibilities. As soon as we arrive at an understanding of the workings of the law of reincarnation, everything begins to fall into place. All of a sudden, everything aligns perfectly. Why are some people poor while others are wealthy, why are some people healthy while others are sick, why are some people worse than others, and so on. For as long as I can remember, I have been amazed by the extraordinary love and perfection that governs our amazing universe. It goes without saying that this is only a very brief summary, and I sincerely hope that you are motivated to learn more about this fascinating topic. That reincarnation was a vital component of the earliest Christian teachings and that it was later forbidden by a Roman Emperor is something that you may not be aware of. No longer is the doctrine of reincarnation taught in any of our churches or other religious organisations. Are you aware that more than fifty percent of people in this globe have faith in the concept of reincarnation. In the United States of America, the founding fathers, Franklin Jefferson, and George Washington all had a strong interest in reincarnation. Additionally, at least a dozen of our presidents, if not more, had the same level of elation. Additionally, the legends of industry such as Thomas Edison, Henry Ford, Paul Getty, and a great number of others in addition to them. The knowledge of the re-embodiment of the soul was also known to the early Christians, which is something that a lot of people are unaware of. There are multiple references to it in the New

Testament. There are passages in the books of Matthew and Mark that describe how Yeshua asks his followers, "Who do the people say that I am?" and they inform him that people believe that he is John the Baptist. Elijah, Jeremiah, or one of the ancient prophets who has returned as Yeshua, and in the book of Matthew, Yeshua explains to some of his disciples on two separate occasions that John the Baptist was the prophet Elijah in a past life. I don't see why Yeshua would educate his disciples about reincarnations. There were many Jews living during that time period who believed in the concept of reincarnation. Yeshua was a Jew, and all of his disciples were also Jews. It was referenced in their ancient mystical text of Kabbalah, which is also known as the Gilgul Neshamot, and it teaches about the soul cycle. Even in modern times, there are a number of Jewish sects that adhere to the doctrine of reincarnation. These include the Chabadniks, the Hasidics, and other Orthodox Jewish communities. From the writings of the early church fathers, such as Origon, we have learned that the concept of reincarnation was well known throughout the Christian community during the first few decades of the religion's existence. However, why is it that this significantly significant aspect of Christ's teaching is no longer acknowledged in the churches that we attend today? So, what took place? It is necessary to travel back in time to the sixth century, to the Eastern Roman Empire, in order to discover the solution to this issue. The Middle East, Italy, Greece, and Turkey, as well as the Mediterranean Region. At the time, the territory that is now known as the Eastern Roman Empire was ruled by a very powerful emperor named Justinian the first. He believed that he was the Supreme Ruler of the Church and the Pope, and he even made it a law that nothing could be done in the Church that was counter to the wish and command of the emperor. He was a true dictator, and he was responsible for dealing with the general war situation in the Eastern Roman Empire as well as the imminent risk of a domestic political religious war in the region that is now known as Palestine. He demanded that everyone adhere to his particular interpretation of the Orthodox faith. In addition, the doctrines of reincarnation were eliminated from the curriculum. He desired for everyone to have faith in a single life and that priests are superior. He also believed that the Church should be seen as the mediators for the salvation of the people. Give it some thought. It was only via the Church that one could reach heaven. It was a potent instrument that might influence the masses. As a result of the pressure exerted by Emperor Justinian the first, the teachings of reincarnation were going to be prohibited in Constantinople, which is now known as Istanbul. This event took place in the year 543. Despite the fact that it took place during the Synod of the Eastern Church, which was a gathering of bishops, Pope Vigilius was aware that it was contrary to the teachings of Christ. As a result, he vehemently resisted the emperor and refused to sign this ban. However, it is impossible for anyone to disagree with an emperor for an extended period of time. As a result, ten years later, on the morning of December 8th, 553, the Pope eventually gave in and made it a law, despite the intense pressure from the Emperor. It was not even brought up during the general council that was held in Constantinople; it was not even addressed. Not at all, but this resulted in a significant issue for the church. The fundamental questions of life were no longer within their ability to explain. We are from where we came from. Why are we being here? After that, where do we go? Therefore, in order to fill the void left by reincarnation, they had to come up with completely new dogmas. For example, they came up with concepts like as the original sin, the creation of the soul at the time of conception, the notion of mortal sin, the concept of the judgement day, purgatory, and the concept of eternal damnation. Jesus did not teach any of this to his disciples.

The First Justinian, however, did not care because, after all, he was the Pope and the ruler of the church, and he was the one who established the regulations. Regrettably, none of the Christian denominations that later broke away from the Catholic Church, such as the Protestants, the Baptists, the Anglican Church, and a thousand other churches, ever sought to rectify this fundamental fault. Nevertheless, the understanding of reincarnation was never lost to history. It has always been taught in the civilizations that were considered to be educated and hidden, and it is currently seeing a new beginning in the Western world. There are an increasing number of Christians in the modern day who are aware of this law and are once again eager to live their lives in accordance with the teachings that Christ initially imparted.

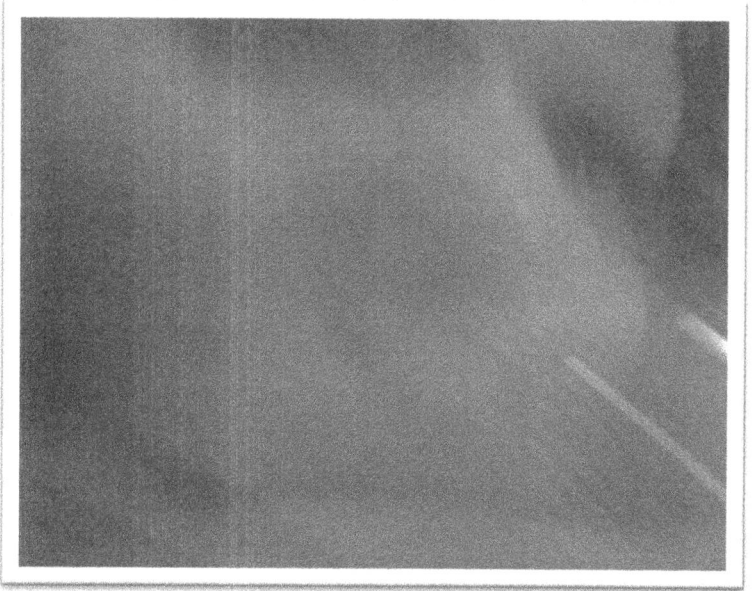

The greatest among you will be the one who comes to know himself.

(Nag Hammadi)

YESHUA

Reincarnation

Having numerous incarnations on earth is not something that is in accordance with the will of God. Why do we do it, and what can we do to put an end to it. Have a look at the splendour that may be found in both nature and in people. Not only is it a human, but it is a community of trillions of cells that work together in complete harmony, symphony, and unity for the purpose of ensuring the health and vitality of the entire body. A cell is an individual, but at the same time, it is completely committed to the welfare of the whole. Bliss, inaction, complete delight, complete harmony, and union comprise this state of being. We are all aware of the consequences that would occur if even a single one of these cells were to proclaim, "I do not want this unity harmony thing." To put myself first, I want my own thing. The term "selfish cell" is widely used to refer to cancer cells, which are cells that are completely hungry and act in a manner that is detrimental to the health of other cells. Their diet consists of other cells, and they frequently eliminate the entire population. In the meantime, let us take a look at the planet Earth, where it is possible to compare humans to a community consisting of eight billion cells, in addition to a few billion earthbound spirits that we are unable to perceive and who remain with their familiars. A human being is a unique and distinct cell that is also a component of a larger group, such as a family, a tribe, or a nation, in the same way that the organs of the body comprise the human body. However, how do all of these many cells and organs that comprise mankind interact with one another. Are many people only looking out for themselves with their own self-centred interests and aspirations, or are they in complete harmony and bliss. In the same way that cancer cells steal energy from one another, we witness them stealing energy from one another through battling, dominating, killing, genocide, and a very long list of other evils. As a result of the planet Earth's evolution into a higher vibration, it is not surprising that our globe is in such a poor shape. Earth as a whole is going to vibrate us pests away. What was the cause of all of this? Where did things go wrong? Which human cells are unable to cooperate with one another? Once upon a time, a group of rebellious divine spiritual beings departed from the absolute truth that we call home and entered the realm of space and time, contrasts, and the relationship between cause and effect. The divine creation was something they wanted to be opposed to, thus they decided to make their own creation. To put it another way, they desired to accomplish it more effectively than Yahweh. There is a distinct possibility that both you and I are among these fallen angels. We entered the world of the relative reality, which consisted of seven spheres capable of providing temporary purification. Because of our activities that were based on ourselves and our own self-interest, we violated the law of love and cast a shadow over our souls, which means that we generated karmic responsibilities for ourselves. As a result of rising negativity, a significant number of us have descended farther and further into the astral material realms, intersecting with planet Earth. We can see that this globe, planet Earth, was given to humanity as a teaching ground for spirits who desired to travel back home, the Absolute Reality. This is something that we can acknowledge. When compared to the spiritual purifying spheres, where the expiation of karma can take a significantly longer amount of time and can also be more painful, souls are able to reverse their karmic burdens and their soul shadows in a relatively short amount of time here on earth. This is because souls do not have the buffer of the physical body. Consequently, the plan was to complete this institute as quickly as possible, and then to climb as a soul that was more cleansed and filled with light, deeper in the purification spheres, all the way back to that place of origin. However, a relatively small number of people have taken advantage of this opportunity to cleanse themselves of their sins during an incarnation. A significant number of us have taken advantage of this moment to go even farther into our own self-centeredness and selfishness, much like the cancer cells. According to the words of Yeshua, "Love thy neighbour as thyself," this earth would have been a paradise if we had used the extremely limited time we have here on earth to practise self-recognition, to cleanse ourselves of our past transgressions, and to develop a more loving and united mindset. On the other hand, a significant number of us have avidly pursued the road of self-centred objectives and desires that bind us to this material world. It is possible that these worldly objectives and wishes will remain here on Earth as vibrational complexes if they are not achieved or satisfied during this lifetime. These complexes can then serve as anchors to pull us back into another incarnation, and then another, and another. Regrettably, a significant number of us have been through hundreds or even thousands of incarnations, but we have not seen much progress in our souls. There is a tendency to remain stagnant within the same group, religion, or culture without making any progress. There is no desire on the part of Yahweh for these endless incarnations to occur repeatedly. To put it another way, it is like going back to our third-grade class over and over again. It would be a silly thing to do, wouldn't it? Through the passage of time, these recurrent incarnations have caused us to become more and more earthbound, rather than "heaven bound" or "homebound" to the location from whence we originally originated. Some individuals are concerned that after they pass away, they will be reincarnated into a different form by a malevolent force or a foreign being. Contrary to popular belief, it is most likely our own unfulfilled desires in the world and our desire for the joys of the physical world that bring us back to the physical world over and over again. However, let's cut to the chase: are we actually having a good time here? Planet Earth appears to be more of a prison for humans than an educational institution, where countries and continents are like prison cells for humanity, each one experiencing its own excruciating collective sin. If we look attentively at all the suffering, we can see that the planet Earth is very similar to a prison. I have gone over this before, but there is one more reason why we ought to make certain that this is the final incarnation that we will ever experience. Because like attracts like, it is a reality that this Earth will very soon evolve into a higher frequency, at which point it will no longer be feasible for souls of lower vibration to incarnate here. This is due to the fact that the frequency of the new Earth will be higher than that of many souls that carry a heavy burden. In the purifying realms, they would next be required to make amends for the sins they had committed. Isn't it wonderful to be aware that we have the ability to put an end to our cycle of reincarnation. Presently, let's get our act together, shall we. It is not necessary for any of us to do it by ourselves. All of the divine beings are on our side, and they are going to assist us in making this work. In the event that we do not choose to return to this world out of love to assist others on their journey back to the light, then this should be our final existence on this planet. Divine revelations on this topic have been bestowed upon us over the course of many years.

We need to hold in our awareness at the time of death in order to escape the wheel of rebirth.

(Nag Hammadi)

"To put off your old self, which belongs to your former manner of life and is corrupt through deceitful desires, and to be renewed in the spirit of your minds, and to put on the new self, created after the likeness of Yahweh in true righteousness and holiness."

(Ephesians 4:22-24)

YESHUA

Life Before Birth

The following is a description of the events that take place when we become incarnate. There are a multitude of reasons why spirits such as ourselves incarnate into the world at this time. There are those who come to heal, those who come to observe, those who come to experience, and those who come to help other souls. On the other hand, the majority of us come here for karmic reasons, which means that we want to undo our karma, plus we want to develop and become more aware of who we truly are. As a result of the fact that souls of varying vibrations and states of consciousness are able to incarnate on planet Earth, this planet serves as an excellent teaching ground for this purpose. When we are in the spiritual world, we are typically surrounded by spirits that have a vibration that is comparable to our own. However, once we are on Earth, we have the opportunity to acquire knowledge, interact with other souls of varying awareness and consciousness, and mix and mingle with them. And in addition to being a very magnificent planet, it is also a really unusual and unique location. We are spiritual beings, souls from our true home, which is the spiritual world, before we go through the process of becoming incarnate. While we are here, we are always learning and growing, but the process of growth is slow paced because we are only surrounded by souls or vibrations that are similar to our own. Additionally, we are in an entirely different environment with a lot of problems, such as here on Earth, which can speed up our process of growing and awakening. Currently, the majority of us have visited this planet a great number of times in the past, and we still maintain karmic connections to other souls that we have interacted with in prior lives. Therefore, when we make the decision to come back to Earth, we consult with our spiritual guide or guides, and there may be additional guides as well, in order to thoroughly organise and discuss our journey. Due to the numerous turns and surprises it is comparable to the bed of a river. There are all of these issues that we face, and we will see all of these hurdles and hardships shown in pictures. Prior to our incarnation, we will reach an agreement with them because we are confident that they will support us in our development and in achieving our goals, and that they will also be of assistance to us during our stay. Some souls with whom we have a very close relationship may also be present. There may be our future earthly mother, father, relative, friend, or spouse, and it is highly probable that we have spent a great deal of time together on earth in the past. It is also possible that we have karmic ties that bind us together at this moment. In addition to resolving our past karma, we also want to cultivate divine qualities such as love, peace, compassion, and mercy once more. For the sake of instance, let us assume that we are afraid that we are, by our very nature, a little bit cold and not as loving as we would like to be, and that we have made the decision that we want to learn love in the lives to come. It is only possible for us to feel attraction to a mother and a father who have a vibration that is comparable to our own, as stated by the universal law of attraction. To put it another way, we would be born to parents who, just like us, struggle to find the right words to communicate their love for us. Just as like attracts like, they both have the same frequency. The vibrational properties that we possess are identical to those that our parents possess. We are going to perform a few simulation births in order to determine whether or not our future bodies are going to be able to fit inside of our mother's stomach. That is always when the baby is kicking in the tummy that they are that they are when the soul is truly in the embryo and trying out if it fits, but the actual birth is the only time when we fully connect and bind with the body. When we take our first breath, the spirit and the body of the individual are brought together. After that, it appears that there is a great deal of dissatisfaction due to the fact that they were born to parents who had a similar vibration. We are now mercilessly reminded of and exposed to a pattern of behaviour that mimics our own character. When we were little children, we would have a strong desire for love and affection, and we would be exposed to the very same environment that we may have provided for our own children in previous lives. Take into consideration the fact that the parents in this incarnation could very well have been our own children in the lives that came before this one. By the time we reach adulthood and become a little bit more mature, the anguish and the absence of love are deeply felt within us as a large void that something is missing. Now, take a look at what occurs to us as we grow older and when we reach adulthood. We will now become the source and spark that flames our passion and our driving force, and this very void of this lack and our childhood will bring about this transformation. We feel a greater sense of emptiness, which in turn increases our desire to make up for it, which in turn increases our level of love. It is therefore possible for children who were raised in homes that were cold to become parents who are very passionate and loving themselves. Furthermore, as a result of their heightened passion or drive, these children are now able to find and offer a great amount of love. Therefore, rather than lamenting the fact that we did not have the perfect and ideal parents or house when we were growing up, we ought to examine what we believe was lacking according to our own perceptions, and then we ought to turn the situation around and allow that energy to become our passion. For example, those who believe they were raised in terrible poverty may acquire a tremendous desire to share their wealth and prosperity with others. What we see to be a deficiency has the potential to become our own driving force. As soon as we have a better understanding of this dynamic, we will no longer hold our parents responsible for our unique development and awakening process; rather, we will express our gratitude to them for providing us with the most ideal environment possible. As time goes on, the spiritual world is providing us with assistance and support to ensure that we are successful in all aspect of our lives.

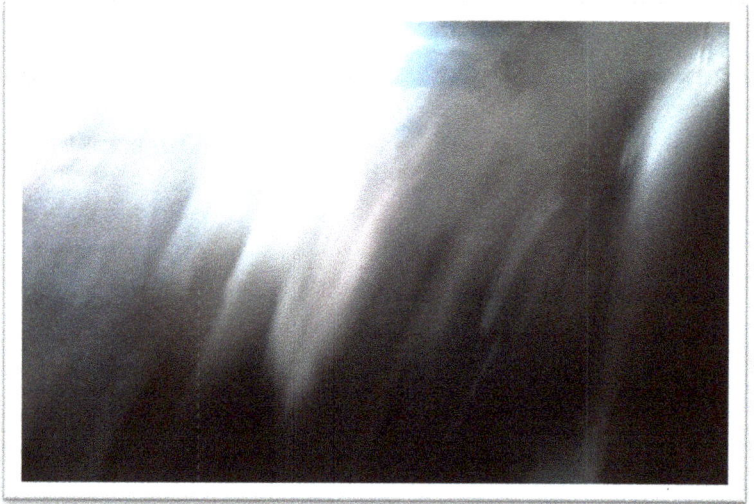

"Recognize what is in your sight, and that which is hidden
from you will become plain to you."

(Nag Hammadi)

YESHUA

Stop Reincarnating

It is not the will of the divine that we continue to incarnate on earth again and over again. It is possible to cease reincarnating if one does not give in to the wants that are based on illusion and instead awakens to the harmony that exists within the absolute reality. The body is used as an example because it is a community of trillions of cells that operate together in complete harmony, symphony, and unity for the purpose of ensuring the health and vitality of the entire body. In spite of the fact that every cell is an individual, it is completely committed to the welfare of the whole, which is bliss in action, complete joy, complete harmony, and complete unity. What would happen if even a single one of these cells decided to say, "I don't want this unity and harmony thing?" is something that we are all aware of. To put myself first, I want my own thing. We would refer to it as a selfish cell, which is also frequently referred to as cancer cells. These cells are completely greedy despite the fact that they are causing harm to other cells. They consume other cells for sustenance and frequently wipe out the entire group. Let us take a look at the planet Earth, where the human race can be compared to a community consisting of eight billion cells, in addition to a few hundreds of billion earthbound spirits that constitute our ethereal selves. Each individual human being is a unique and distinct cell that is also a component of a bigger group, such as a family, a tribe, a nation, and just like the organs that make up the human body. However, how is it that all of these cells and organs that comprise mankind are able to work together in complete harmony and absolute happiness, just like our body is able to do? Or do many people simply have their own self-interests and goals in mind, always looking out for themselves? In the same way that cancer cells steal energy from one another, we observe them stealing energy from one another through acts of violence, dominance, killing, genocide, and a variety of other evils. Considering that our planet is ready to grow into a higher frequency, it is not surprising that our world is in such a poor situation. Planet Earth is preparing to shake us parasites. In what way did all of this take place, what went wrong, and why are these human cells unable to cooperate with one another? Since the beginning of time, there have been divine spiritual beings that have departed from the absolute truth, which is our home, and have entered the realm of space and time opposites, as well as cause and effect. The divine creation was something they wanted to be opposed to, thus they decided to make their own creation. They intended to accomplish it in a manner that was superior to that of Yahweh. There is a distinct possibility that both you and I are among these fallen angels. We entered the world of the relative reality, which consisted of seven spheres capable of providing temporary purification. Because of our activities that were centred on ourselves and our own self-interest, we violated the law of love and cast a shadow over our souls, which means that we generated karmic responsibilities for ourselves. As the level of negativity in our lives increased, a significant number of us descended further and further into the astral and material universes, along with the planet earth. We can see that this planet, planet earth, was given to humanity as a place for souls that desired to return back to the absolute reality. This is something that we can see. As opposed to the spiritual purifying spheres, where the expiation of karma can take considerably longer and can also be more painful due to the fact that souls do not have the buffer of the physical body, here on earth, souls are able to remove their karmic burdens and their soul shadows in a relatively short amount of time. The objective was to cleanse oneself and travel through this location, and then to climb as a more purified and enlightened soul deeper in the purification spheres all the way back to one's own home. During an incarnation, however, only a small percentage of people have taken advantage of this opportunity to discharge their karma. Along the same lines as the cancer cells, many of us have taken advantage of this opportunity to sink even more into our own self-centeredness and selfishness. According to the words of Yeshua, "love thy neighbour as thyself," if we had invested our extremely limited time on earth in self-recognition, in resolving our past karma, and in developing a more loving and united mindset, we would have been able to do all of these things. On this planet, paradise would have been the result. On the other hand, a significant number of us have avidly pursued the road of self-centred objectives and desires that bind us to this material world. These worldly objectives and wants will linger here on earth as vibrational complexes if they are not achieved or satisfied in this lifetime. These complexes can then work as anchors to pull us back into another incarnation, and then another, and another, and another. Regrettably, a significant number of us have been through hundreds or even thousands of incarnations, but we have not seen much progress in our souls. There is a tendency to remain stagnant within the same group, religion, or culture without making any progress. There is no desire on the part of Yahweh for these endless incarnations to occur repeatedly. We are going through the motions of our third-grade class over and over again. That would be a stupid assumption, because over the course of time, these reincarnations have rendered us more and more earthbound rather than heaven bound, a home bound to the place from where we once originated. Despite the fact that this is not the case, there are some individuals who are concerned that after they pass away, they will be reincarnated by a malevolent entity or a foreign being. The most likely reason why we find ourselves drawn back into physicality again and over again is because of our own unfulfilled desires in the world and our need to experience pleasures in our bodies. Nevertheless, let's be honest, are we truly having a good time in this place. When we take a closer look at all of the suffering that is occurring on earth, we see that it is more like a jail for humans than a pleasant place. Countries and continents are like prison cells for humanity, and each one is facing its own collective karma, which may be excruciating. I have discussed this before, but there is one more reason why we ought to make certain that this is the final incarnation that we will ever experience. Like attracts like, and the new earth frequency will be greater than that of many souls that are carrying heavy burdens. It is a reality that very soon this Earth will evolve into a higher frequency, and when this occurs, it will no longer be feasible for souls with lower vibrations to incarnate here. In the purification realms, they will be required to make up for the karmic debts they have accumulated. It would be preferable for a soul to avoid reincarnation. It is not necessary for any of us to do it by ourselves. All of the divine beings are on our side, and they are going to assist us in making this work. Let this be our final existence on earth, unless we have a strong desire to return to this world out of love to help others find their way back to the light. Through the years, the divine has provided us with a great deal of revelations regarding this topic, as well as through his word and Yeshua.

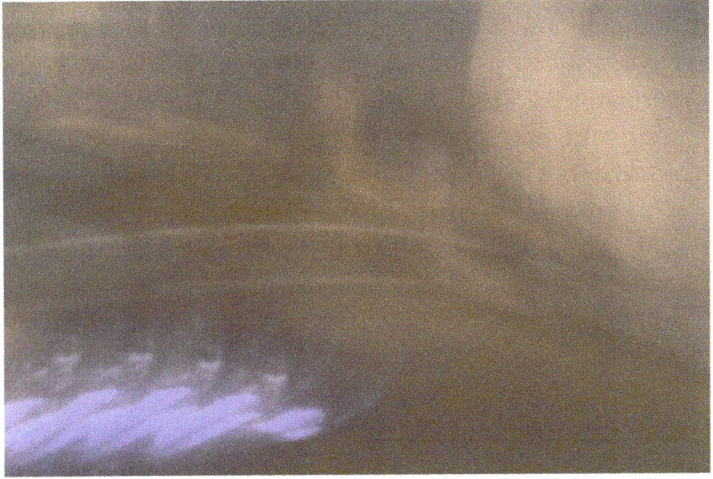

Those who seek should not cease seeking until they find.
When they find, they will be disturbed. When they are
disturbed, they will marvel.

(Nag Hammadi)

YESHUA

Baby Soul

I want to put forward the traditional belief systems that we have, as well as investigate and discuss a more profound comprehension of the spiritual laws. The experience of a soul as a newborn baby is going to be the focus of my discourse. This is a continuation of the chapter I wrote about life before birth, which goes into detail about the events that take place before we make our physical appearance. According to what we have been told in the past, we are spiritual beings or souls that incarnate here on earth, mostly for the purpose of fulfilling our karmic obligations. From this point forward, we have a soul in the spiritual realm, and here on earth, we have a mother and father who are expecting a child. Now, the selection of parents is not a random occurrence; rather, it is the result of meticulous planning and mutual agreement between the soul and the next generation of parents. Additionally, there must be a vibratory similarity between the soul and the mother-to-be who is expecting a child. Similar things tend to attract one another. We can also make the assumption that the soul and the parents-to-be have been together in prior lives, and that this has occurred a great number of times. For the first time, the soul makes contact with the embryo that is still inside the mother by a vibrational response. When this occurs, the soul basically puts out its feelers and adjusts its radiation to the genes, the genetic tendencies of the future body. In certain instances, the soul alone influences the genes to develop an ill or even disabled body in order to give the ideal vehicle for unburdening karma. When the embryo continues to develop inside the womb of the mother, the soul moves closer to the mother and the unborn child during the course of the pregnancy. The soul will frequently enter the embryo for a brief period of time in order to test it out. This is the only time that the mother is able to feel the baby kicking inside of her abdomen, and it only happens at the moment of birth. The soul forms a connection with the infant with the very first breath or cry. At the pituitary gland, it is located, which is where it finds its home. One of the tiny structures that can be found at the base of the brain. At this point, you might be wondering how a fully developed soul and a soul that has reached maturity can suddenly become so small that it can fit inside the cranium of a young child. The structure of the soul is where the secret begins to be found. Our soul is composed of spiritual particles that wrap into each other in this manner, whereas our physical body is composed of cells. It is also possible to conceive of the rose, but in this case, all of the petals are folded into each other, and then they eventually spread out into complete blossoms. While it takes some time, the spirit will eventually feel completely at ease in this new, smaller body. Just for a moment, try to picture yourself being abruptly crammed into this meagre body. The process of completely bonding might take weeks, months, and even years to complete. It is during this period that the soul continues to live very much under the influence of the spiritual realm from where it originated, and numerous times throughout sleep, it returns to this world in order to renew itself. In his most recent book, titled Before He Died, Wayne Dyer has written about the remarkable memories that children have of periods of their lives that occurred before they were born on earth. Memories of Heaven is the name of this book. It is reasonable to suppose that the soul and the infant not only recall their time spent in the spiritual world, but also their prior lives spent on earth. This is because the number of souls that incarnate here for the first time is quite low. An incredible amount of research was conducted on this topic by Dr. Ian Stevenson of the University of Virginia School of Medicine. He conducted interviews with more than three thousand children from all over the world, as well as recorded and researched their memories of their previous lives. Therefore, it may take several weeks, months, or even years until the individual's spirit is entirely engulfed in a veil of perfect oblivion. This means that beyond a certain point in our existence, we are no longer able to remember our previous incarnations or our lives in the spiritual world. In spite of this, we are able to recall everything for as long as we are contained within this little newborn body. A fully developed awareness is looking back at us from behind the eyes of the little infant that we are holding in our arm. This indicates that the soul of the baby has made a contract with us as its guardians or parents a very long time ago, before we were ever born. Adoptive parents are also included in this category, and it is highly probable that we have been together with that for a great number of lives previously. An infant possesses a level of entire consciousness that is comparable to that of an adult in some respects. People frequently have the misconception that a child's mind is fresh, or that it is as fresh and blank as the body itself, but this is not the case. The only part of the brain that is fresh is the physical one, but the mind is very old, and a soul is already there inside the newborn. That has been a mistake on numerous occasions in the past and is still well conscious of this fact. Try to picture yourself. The only thing you can remember is the lovely weightlessness of your spiritual body before you incarnated, and you could recall the last time you were here on earth, which could have been millennia ago. You are so trapped in this newborn body that you never remember anything else. Now, all of a sudden, you find yourself in a completely new and foreign historical period, confronted with various standards and ways of thinking, with different ideas, habits, traditions, and the curiosities of the people who are surrounding you. How would you feel at this moment? In the baby's soul, this is a significant change that needs to be made. As a result, it is imperative that it be safeguarded and not intentionally subjected to any form of injury. This covers situations that are horrifying and excruciating, such as circumcision. It is disheartening to observe the number of children who are raised in households where their parents are constantly arguing and fighting with one another, or who are part of a family that is filled with discord, a lack of joy, and inner pain. Infants have a sensitive soul that is able to register everything. The soul is able to perceive everything, regardless of whether the infant is awake or asleep. Not only is it able to read and comprehend our ideas, but it can also recall what thoughts are. The energy that we constantly emit into the world is referred to as our thoughts. It is true that we think in pictures, and these pictures or images of pictures leave us and end up as thought formations that surround us and can be picked up by individuals who are sensitive. In the same way that a sponge is susceptible to all vibrations, the brain cells of a newborn baby are generally unburdened and will thus be receptive to any and all vibrations. As parents or guardians, it is our responsibility to assist this soul in readjusting to this three-dimensional physical reality in a gentle and loving manner. This is because the brain of the infant is absorbing all of these concepts from the people who are surrounding them, regardless of whether they are sleeping or awake. Give you an explanation. At the outset, we always select our parents in accordance with our vibrations and the soul contracts that we established. In the second place, the soul forms a connection with a new infant body after delivery, beginning with the first breath and the first cry. The third point is that the soul is not a new soul; rather, it is a fully grown soul that is still able to remember its life in the spiritual realm as well as its prior lives. This can continue for weeks, months, or even years, and fourthly, it is our responsibility to assist this soul in readjusting to the three-dimensional physicality that exists in our world while ensuring that it is safeguarded from any harm.

Whoever has come to understand the world has found only a corpse, and whoever has found a corpse is superior to the world.

(Nag Hammadi)

When one gains this insight, they transcend the attachments and illusions of the material world, gaining a sense of superiority or detachment from its ephemeral nature.

(Nag Hammadi)

YESHUA

Possession

This chapter discusses earthbound spirits, which are also referred to as lost souls. These spirits have the ability to inhabit certain individuals and make their life extremely difficult. If you have never heard of this topic before, you are going to find that it contains some extremely interesting facts. Being possessed by spirits is as old as humanity itself. We find descriptions and stories of spirit possessions in every culture, but the most renowned of these are the numerous references in the Bible to Yeshua helping people by driving out unclean spirits. You may find these references throughout the Bible. Somewhere near twenty-one references are included. Who exactly are these possessive souls, and why are they such an issue to society as a whole. The vast majority of them are persons who have passed away physically and are unable to comprehend or acknowledge the fact that they have passed away physically and that they are now in the spiritual body. Leaving the physical world and entering this spiritual world is a relatively straightforward process that occurs after death. This is like to moving from one room to another room or travelling from one country to another country. When we pass away, we will continue to live, but not in the physical body but in the spiritual body, and this has nothing to do with the religious beliefs that we have. How that mother nature has been functioning for millions of years is just like this. On the other hand, there are individuals who are quite certain that when they pass away, there will be complete and utter extinction. When these individuals pass away, they just are unable to accept the truth that they have passed away physically and that they are still living. There is no such thing as an afterlife. It is not consistent with their belief system, and the same is true for those who adhere to extremely traditional or religious dogmatic beliefs and are unable to acknowledge the existence of death. To put it another way, our beliefs determine how we interpret the world around us. When these souls with these powerful thoughts pass away, they are extremely perplexed, and we refer to them as lost souls. They are not open to any teachings or any direction from light beings, who are typically there to welcome them before they pass away. To explain this point, let me give you a typical example. Let's imagine we have a young male for example who enjoys drinking and going out to parties. Due to the fact that he is still young and believes that he is unbreakable, it is normal for him to not be concerned with mortality or even believe that there is life after death. In most cases, young individuals do not behave in that manner. At this point, he is drinking a few beers after work, and while he is driving home, he is involved in a vehicle accident. He passes away quickly, and his soul is expelled from his body. He now possesses a spiritual body that, to him, is just as real as the physical one he no longer possesses. His cerebral and emotional faculties are also very much unchanged, and because he does not believe that life exists after the physical death, he considers himself to be quite fortunate to have survived the accident. During the moment when he passed away physically, light beings from the spiritual realm, along with possibly some loved ones who had passed away in the past, arrived to greet him and lead him to the spiritual worlds. Nevertheless, even if he does see them, he will disregard them all and run away from them since his worldview does not allow for them to exist. He might be under the impression that they are nothing more than ghosts, but the vehicle accident might have impacted him like an immense amount of concrete, and his first reaction might be, "I need another drink." Having this thinking alone is sufficient to bring him to the nearest pub or other place where he can drink. In the beginning, he may be astonished or even upset that everyone seems to ignore him since he is invisible to them. However, he will quickly realise that he can satisfy his alcohol addiction by interacting with another human being who has a similar weakness or addiction, which means that they have a similar soul vibration. As the saying goes, "like attracts like," and here we have a person who fits that description seated at the bar. This is in full compliance with the law. At this moment, this earthbound soul lurches upon this guest, enters his aura and his body, and then proceeds to enjoy his drink through him. Currently, he is a soul that possesses other things. There is nothing romantic about vampires, despite the fact that writers have romanticised such souls as supernatural beings. On the contrary, they are quite dangerous and frequently wicked, and from this point on, this lost soul will possess, influence, and control this human being through the use of their thoughts. This lost soul will now continue to project thoughts and urges of drinking, eating, or doing drugs, or seeing more pornographic content, or whatever it is that turns the possessed soul on. The human person will be convinced that these are his own thoughts, but in reality, they are not his own thoughts. They originate from the soul that is occupying people, which is yet another heartbreaking fact. It is extremely uncommon for a single lost soul to have complete control over or possess a single individual. A number of other lost souls who are also addicted to the substance will become attached to it. Very soon, there will be a great number of additional ones, similar to clusters of grapes, that are attached to this one mortal being. They will follow him about wherever he goes and exert their influence on him like a puppet. Similar to sponges, they consume the vitality of the person they are living with. It is not only that spirits enter because of their addiction; they also sometimes do so for the purpose of exacting retribution, and they have the ability to even push their victim to commit suicide and, in certain instances, murder. However, in order for it to take place, the host must initially exhibit some form of emotional pattern that corresponds to the situation. Hospitals, in addition to bars and other places where people are addicted to substances, are another area where spirits can readily inhabit the bodies of other people. Once more, there are a great number of individual souls who have lately passed on but are unable to accept their new circumstances. While they are wandering around the hospital, they come across another patient or a visitor who has a vibration that is like to their own. They then slide into the aura and body of the other person, where they continue to live through them. While we are on the subject of hospitals, another risk associated with spirit transplants occurs during organ transplant sessions. These lost spirits are also known to enter babies or small children and in such cases, it is the similar vibrating emotional imbalance of one of the parents of the child or baby that attracts such a vagabonding soul and besides hospitals, graveyards, funeral homes, prisons and mental institutions, there is one other easy entry for such souls, and that are people who are consciously inviting spirits to speak or express themselves through them and I'm speaking of seances, ouija boards, planchettes, automatic writings, channellings and so on. Souls are invited to participate in all of these activities; but there is no assurance that only souls that are virtuous or highly advanced will be drawn to them. There are no lost souls, and even former souls are thrilled by these invitations. They are eager to move in and dwell with whoever invites them, and they also adore these invitations. At this point, let us take a look at a few signs or consequences that can point to the presence of a possessive spirit. An abrupt shift in personality or state of well-being, or a behaviour that is erratic and impulsive, such as excessive weariness, depression, or extreme tiredness, is frequently the cause of this condition. It is true that occupying spirits can have a variety of causes; nonetheless, the majority of the time, they are responsible for draining the vitality of the hosts and causing abrupt and serious mental difficulties. The minds of their hosts are being manipulated and influenced by these lost spirits, who are masters of the situation. Consider the cases of schizophrenia or the violent outbursts of fury, as well as the mental hospitals or prisons that are available. Alcoholism and drug addiction as well. There are many indications of spirit possession, but these are some of the more damaging ones. In addition, this can involve issues related to weight and obesity, as well as addictions to smoking. These spirits bring their cravings with them and ensure that any attempts to diet will be unsuccessful. Additionally, they cause problems in relationships since they cause couples to suddenly have a menage à trois without their knowledge or agreement, which results in problems. Spirit possession can lead to a variety of sexual issues, including sexual uncertainty, sexual addictions, and sexual disorders. Not only in the bedroom, but also in other areas of our lives, we are facing significant challenges in the event that the male spirit enters a female or vice versa. There are instances in which it can result in homosexuality; nevertheless, the majority of the time, transvestites or transgender people are the result of a powerful occupying spirit of the opposing sex within them. I would like to make it perfectly clear that I do not intend to in any way, shape, or form imply that possessive spirit is always the source of these problems. To the contrary. However, in her book titled "The Unquiet Dead," the physician Edith Fiori asserts that seventy percent of her patients genuinely possessed the spirit of the dead. Everyone who is living in a vibratory world that is comparable to the world of ideas, feelings, emotions, and desires that is possessed by spirits has the potential to become a victim of those spirits. One approach to get free of spirits is to love and honour oneself, as well as to work through addictions and emotional injuries. It is, however, too late for many people to have been puppets of these invaders for a considerable amount of time. For further information on the various methods that can be utilised by them to liberate and expel these occupying spirits, I would like to recommend the numerous books that have been authored by medical professionals and specialists in this subject. There are books that provide evidence that spirit possession is a spiritual occurrence that is supported by medical studies and accounts.

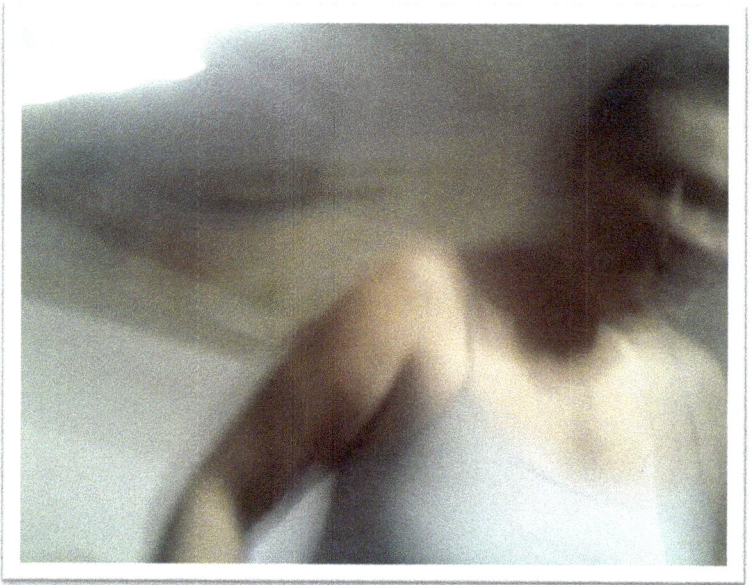

Whoever does not seek the kingdom while he is alive will
not be able to seek it after death.

(Nag Hammadi)

YESHUA

Suicide

It is not as uncommon as one might believe to have thoughts about ending one's own life. Many people have thought about it at one time or another in their lives, and as human beings see on earth, we sometimes go through situations which seemed to be unbearable or even hopeless and it's only natural for us to have the desire to escape these situations and if you find yourself in such a predicament or know somebody who is struggling with thoughts of suicide, allow me to share with you the spiritual perspective, because that's what we are. In this physical world, we are spiritual beings who are experiencing time and space for the first time. Let's get a better understanding of what occurs to our souls before we arrive on Earth. In this life, we were blessed with the opportunity to incarnate on the planet Earth; however, prior to our birth, we engaged in conversations and made plans on the fundamental aspects of our lives that would take place in this world. Together with our spiritual guides, we were able to accomplish this. What we were interested in learning was discussed in our future lives, to either heal or provide to others. This will be our life on Earth in the future, and in accordance with our own goals, we have made certain that certain conditions are established that will allow us to take advantage of these chances. You see, our future lives were not planned out like a riverbed, and the rapids, turns, and twists that we encounter are the challenges or obstacles that we face in order to grow, to serve others, or to heal ourselves. When we are here on Earth, we have to use our free will in order to successfully overcome and master these obstacles. Therefore, prior to our birth, we have made a conscious decision to experience the situation that will challenge us and cause us to grow. It was with great affection that we crafted them for ourselves. Even though we are aware that these experiences can be very challenging, we have wholeheartedly agreed to them for the sake of our soul and the purpose of our journey here on earth. In some instances, we may even have made a contract with another soul who loves us very much to incarnate with us here on earth. This is because we wanted them to be beneficial to our soul and to fulfil the purpose of our journey for the sake of encouraging us, for us here, for example, for the purpose of providing us with these challenging situations or for our own personal development and growth. After we have arrived on Earth, we have no recollection of all of this or any of the challenges that we faced. The problem that we are forced to deal with appears to come out of nowhere, and we frequently experience a sense of being victimised by them. But all of these difficulties were pre-arranged by us, and if we were to commit suicide right now, we would be breaking all of these agreements. We are aware that everything that we do in life has repercussions, and in the case of suicide, these consequences are simple, to begin with. As we have come here to earth to learn, our lessons here on earth are cut short through suicide. The completion of this instruction will require us to return at some point in the future. What this means is that we have to start the entire process over again; we have to be born again, we have to grow up in an environment that is comparable to the one we strive to avoid, and we have to finally face the very same challenge that we are trying to avoid. We would not be compelled to return to our seats to complete our class. If we were to experience the same option point and make a different selection because we are aware that it will be to our advantage, this would be an example of our own free will and desire. Secondly, as human beings, we are never given more than we are able to eat. This is something that we experience. There is usually a correlation between the challenges we are facing and the strength that we possess. Despite the fact that we may believe that the current circumstances are beyond our capacity to endure, this is not the case. As a general rule, we are usually far stronger than we believe ourselves to be, and we are able to pull through this. One of the most wonderful aspects is that we do not have to do it by ourselves. To put it simply, the spiritual realm is more than happy to assist us. No matter if we inquire with Yahweh, Yeshua, or our guardian spirit in this place. It makes no difference, and all of our supporters are on our side. All we need to do is make a request. On the other hand, let us not beg for a certain result; rather, let us merely ask for direction and strengths. What manner in which Yahweh will assist us is left up to Yahweh. Because he is aware of the wider picture, he is constantly aware of what will be most beneficial for us. Always keep in mind the words, "Thy will be done to me." Let's give in to these words and surrender. Take some time to reflect about these words. Please allow them to resonate through us. They have an incredible amount of power. The possibility of entering a state of purgatory is the third consequence that can befall a soul that has committed suicide. Let me tell you, this is a fascinating condition of being awake. This is the location where the soul might be hanging on in the spiritual realm till the actual day of the death that was originally intended, which is here, most likely would take place. This can be a very solitary, tiring, and uninteresting period of time. We will have to confront that; in addition, we will find ourselves on the other side, and the energy of all the problems that we intended to get away from are still with us. The fourth consequence is that our suicide will do harm to other people. Do we want to face that? They would experience feeling sad and heartbroken. To the extent that our acts have an impact on the world around us, or the suffering and anguish that we cause to other people by taking our own lives, we will have a profound sense of remorse on the other side. Let us take a look at the challenging scenario that we are currently facing. It is possible that we believe it to be hopeless; yet, can we be certain that this is the case? Give it some thought. Do we have any way of knowing for certain that things will not alter in the future? Because change is the only thing that is consistent in this universe, it follows that no circumstance, not even the most hopeless one, will remain unchanged. There is a possibility that we may feel as though we are descending down a deep valley, and the darkness will continue to increase; but we will ultimately reach the lowest point, and then we will climb uphill towards the light once more. Have we ever pondered the reason that Yahweh made it possible for us to arrive on this earth? The gift that Yahweh bestowed upon us is the gift of life here on earth. We must not throw it back in his face because it is spiritually significant. We are a great spiritual being that was formed in the image of Yahweh, and we are surrounded by spiritual beings who really love us and are happy to support us and assist us in any situation they want us to succeed in. They want us to be successful. They are on our side in this conflict. Let us follow their lead and enable them to lead us through this time. It will come as a surprise to us how much stronger and wiser we have gotten, and we will be amazed by ourselves. In the event that we are successful in overcoming this obstacle, we will be in a position to provide those who are on the point of giving up the strength and hope they need.

If you bring forth what is within you, what you bring forth will save you. If you do not bring forth what is within you, what you do not bring forth will destroy you.

(Nag Hammadi)

YESHUA

Karma

We should never elevate our voices in opposition to our karma. Refrain from complaining when life presents us with difficulties, difficulties, and sorrow. Learning how to alter it is a better option. Educate yourself on how to negotiate your karma. To begin the process of negotiating karma, the first step is to refrain from engaging in detrimental activities. When we do things, we are all aware that they are wrong. We are aware that it is inappropriate to criticise, cuss, or speak negatively about other people. When we treat one another poorly, we are aware that this is wrong. Despite this, we do. We have a sense of justification. To our way of thinking, this is our right. In our opinion, the suffering of others is deserved. When someone accuses us, we lash out in anger. We feel envious of the appearance of other people. When we are in the right, we feel a sense of pride. There is a fear that we will be found out at some point. We are always, from moment to moment, in a state of stress because we are so under the influence of hidden motivations and urges, and we are continuously running from one event to the next, from one scene to the next, always with the subtly held belief that we will somehow be able to get away with carrying out all of these criminal acts. On the scale, our acts and the effects of our activities are what are being evaluated, not our intentions. Therefore, rather than relying just on our good intentions, we need to be aware of how to behave in an appropriate manner. Always behave in the same manner that you would like to be treated. You will establish a circle of actions and consequences if you treat other people well. If you want to be treated well, you must treat other people well. The main method for negotiating karma is to refrain from engaging in detrimental behaviours and instead engage in helpful ones. If someone has wronged you and done something that you regard to be truly bad, then the appropriate course of action may be to forgive them, love them, and assist them without passing judgement on them or attempting to convey to them what you think of them. Gandhi's life serves as a remarkable illustration of the kind of deliberate activity that can be seen in this category. As a result of the huge upheaval that was taking place in India, the Hindus and Muslims were shooting and killing each other. This was a civil war that was extremely nasty and brutal, and it resulted in the deaths and injuries of a great number of individuals. In order to demonstrate his disapproval of the situation, Gandhi abstained from eating and fasting. He did this because he was aware that all of them were incapable of listening to reason because they were so driven by intense hatred and wrath. People ultimately responded to his protest and stopped fighting and murdering, and a large number of people came to visit him laying on his bed, nearly dead from a lack of food. This was despite the fact that he was a Hindu, and he was well-liked by both Muslims and Hindus. So, people eventually responded to his protest. A man who identified as Hindu approached him with tears of regret and confessed that he had realised he had committed awful acts. He stated that he had been responsible for the deaths of a large number of Muslims, as well as women and children. The man expressed profound regret and inquired about the ways in which he could ever make amends for his actions. Gandhi was aware that he was receptive to hearing what he had to say since he felt such profound regret and acknowledged that he was accountable. Consequently, Gandhi instructed the Hindu man to locate a Muslim youngster who was without a parent, adopt him as his own child, and bring him up. With a great deal of gratitude, the man enthusiastically agreed to this. However, Gandhi responded by saying, "Wait, that is not all; you must continue to raise him as a Muslim." The Hindu guy was, of course, taken aback by this discovery, to bring up a child of his adversary in accordance with the practices of his adversary. Obviously, this was the appropriate course of action to take. The use of forceful action results in powerful outcomes. In order to triumph over powerful effects, one must engage in behaviours that are even more powerful. Be sure to keep in mind that a superior action triumphs over a subpar action. The most significant forms of action are those that involve significant acts of sacrifice, in which we give up our own interests and goals in order to better serve the needs of other people. This is the appropriate course of action. This constitutes mindful behaviour. This exemplifies the concept of sacrifice and serves as a compelling model for all of us to emulate. Keep in mind, however, that sacrifice means that we give up something. For the sake of a child and as a form of retribution for his wrongdoings, the Hindu man who served as our example was going to be required to give up a great deal, including his social image, his pride, his vanity, and his own religion. Through all of these efforts, beginning with the moment-to-moment effort to monitor yourself, to be conscious of everything you do, and to be watching the mind very attentively, you are sending a message to your inner being that you are willing to change. If you show via your actions that you are prepared to give up your desires, comforts, and conveniences in order to serve the greater good, then your Innermost will be able to negotiate your karma on your behalf, and as a result, you will obtain what you require to continue working towards the resolution of your responsibilities. They will gradually awaken consciousness until they are capable of another level of karma negotiation, which is direct negotiation in the Temple of Karma. Those who are sincere about activating the three components in their moment-to-moment experience will gradually awaken consciousness. If a pupil has achieved a sufficient level of consciousness awakening, they will be able to acquire the privilege to visit the Temple of Karma in the Astral Plane, which is located outside of their physical body, and negotiate with Anubis and the Lords of Karma in order to request assistance or reward. Doing nice things is necessary if we are to pay back what we owe. As long as we are under the influence of craving, aversion, and ignorance, we will not be able to carry out acts of kindness. The source of misery is desire. Deprive oneself of desire in order to be liberated from misery. Those creatures who are liberated from the shackles of desire are able to liberate themselves from all forms of servitude and are able to perform magnificent actions for the benefit of all other beings. Nevertheless, people who are oppressed by their desires are the ones who bring suffering to others. The purpose of karma is to rid us of our desires. Our karma is sent to us by the One Law as a medication for our own good, to deliver us from the evils that we have committed against ourselves. This is done with a great deal of compassion for the consciousness. The purpose of our suffering is to teach us something. They are there because Yahweh has compassion on them and wants to give them another opportunity to strive for perfection. This is the reason why the beings that suffer in hell are there. As a result of the One Law, the creations of desire are punished. Unfortunately, when the formations of desire are punished, the consciousness undergoes suffering. This occurs when the consciousness is locked inside the structures of desire. You have the ability to make a request for assistance to the law. The legislation may provide the consciousness with aid, benefits, credits, and other forms of assistance. Having said that, nothing is free. It is necessary for us to rid ourselves of any and all ego in order to achieve harmony with the law. It is the One Law that stands in opposition to the creations of desire. The forms of desire are created as a consequence of our deeds in the past; they are our own karma, and they cause us to experience sorrow. A person must become an embodiment of the law in order to achieve total harmony with the law. There is more to karma than the concept of good and evil; it is the equilibrium of actions. All that is good contains elements of evil, and all that is evil has elements of good. Good and evil are not relevant to the gods. Love, which is the law, is one of the gods' core values. Karma can be defined as conscious love in action.

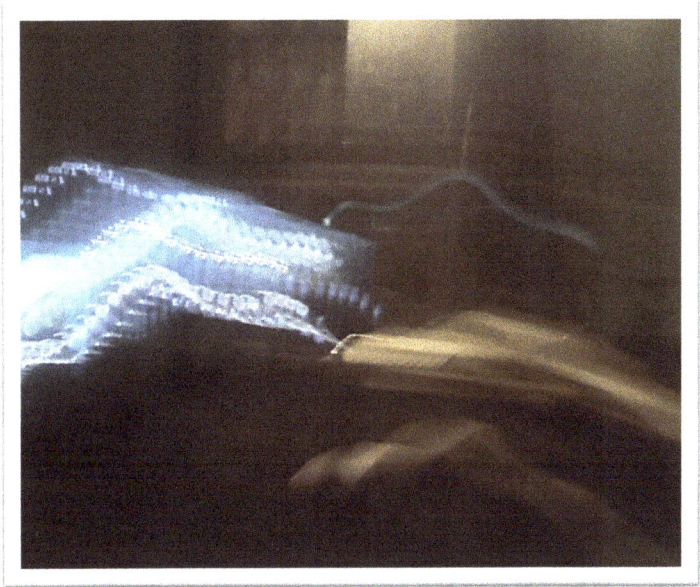

The Father's Kingdom is spread out upon the earth, and men do not see it.

(Nag Hammadi)

YEHSUA

Forgiveness

Karma is a form of medicine that, for our own benefit, is given to us. We would be in a lot more dire situation than we are right now if there were no such thing as karma. However, because there are repercussions for the activities that we choose, we are held accountable and we are compelled to acquire knowledge. We gain knowledge by experiencing the repercussions of activity that is harmful to us and by being rewarded for acts that are helpful to us. This does not negate the fact that karma can be broken. In the same way that we are able to forgive others for their debts, the divine is also able to forgive us for ours. One of the most precious gems in the crown of consciousness is forgiveness. Karma is not a law that is all-knowing and uncaring. But if that were the case, Yahweh would not show mercy. Conversely, Yahweh is merciful. In point of fact, love is the law, and indeed, Yahweh is love. Although karma may appear to be harsh, bitter, or even cruel, it is just what we require in order to look within ourselves and discover the truth. Sugar is not the flavour of the medicine that is meant to heal the soul. The fact remains that it is offered out of love. When there is complete and total repentance, there is no need for punishment. The process of renunciating harmful activities becomes effortless when we have a complete understanding of the suffering that is created by behaviours that are detrimental. After that, we will be able to eliminate the emotional origin of those desires to engage in destructive behaviour. If the cause of the injury is no longer present within ourselves, then there is no need for us to be punished. As a result of the fact that a person who does not have anger cannot become furious, there is no requirement to punish the individual for their anger. When it is determined that we are no longer capable of perpetrating the offence, forgiveness is granted. In order for us to be forgiven, we need to rid ourselves of the aspects that wish to engage in harmful behaviours. On the other hand, if we continue to harbour the desire to do the offence, we do not merit forgiveness. We need to proceed through three distinct levels of observation, judgement, and removal in order to achieve purification from any potentially damaging emotional factor. It is not fair to forgive or show pity to the destructive aspects that are present in us. They are the source of suffering, and they are the only ones who can bring about suffering. Getting clear of them is necessary. During the process of observation, we pay particular attention to the manner in which the element strives to exert its impact on our three brains, the intellect (conscious thoughts), the heart (emotions), and the body (impulses and cravings). The practice of collecting facts, as opposed to theories or speculations, is what observation is all about. During observation, only the facts are thought upon. An observation that only obtains data through the five senses of the physical body is similar to a prosecutor who does not have any evidence from the site of the wrongdoing. The intellectual environment is where the act took place in us. Therefore, it is necessary for us to collect behavioural proof. To put it another way, we need to pay attention to the facts of our thoughts, feelings, and impulses as they actually occurred. It is necessary for us to collect data in two different ways in order for this to be effective. The first method is to observe the element that is active within us at each given instant. The second method is to properly review the scene of action, which is a technique that is similar to meditation. Unless we make a conscious effort to observe ourselves from moment to moment, we will not be able to collect the information necessary to understand how our intellectual apparatus functions. We are unable to comprehend the mental state and inner origins of those aspects unless we engage in intense meditation on the acts of those elements. When we go about our daily lives, we need to make sure that meditation and observation go hand in hand. For observation to be effective, it must be active, awake, and ongoing. In order to meditate well, one must be completely at peace, completely detached from the outside world, and able to see things in a way that is really clear. There is just one objective that both meditation and observation share, and that is to gather knowledge. For the practices of observation and meditation to be successful, they must be devoid of any emotional impact or influence from any other source. To put it another way, our perspective must be the result of a free and unconditioned mind that observes without any pride, shame, envy, lust, yearning, aversion, gluttony, greed, laziness, or any other form of self-will. After we have acquired enough evidence for analysis, we will be able to evaluate the component and find it to be unacceptable. Judgement takes place when we are convinced of the wrongdoing and the cause of the offence, and when at the same time, remorse develops naturally. We are said to have comprehended the element when we are unable to act on the impulses that it possesses. When we suddenly encounter the person or thing that we were angry at, we start to feel love for them instead of hate. This is an example of an element of rage that we can understand. This demonstrates that the aspect of anger that had previously managed to exert an influence on us is no longer able to do so and is now prepared to be eradicated. The divinity is the one who bestows elimination. The Divine, who is both the mother and father of the divine presence inside us, is responsible for the elimination of karmic forms. Those individuals who do not erase their spiritual karma by eliminating them of their own free will, will be subjected to purification in hell. Persephone, also known as Hekate, is the goddess of the underworld, and she is in charge of overseeing the purification of conditioned consciousness. Consequently, the divine mother and father purifies us of our transgressions, whether we choose to do so throughout our everyday lives here and now or whether we choose to do so without our choice while we are falling into hell after death. We would be better off if we did it on our own. This is a great action that results in a variety of significant advantages. Among these advantages is the fact that Yahweh has the ability to forgive us of a wide variety of karma. Our mother and father, who love us very much, are both members of the divine. Yahweh does not wish for us to be in a state of suffering.

Blessed are they who have known God in a body, for their
sight and their mind remain whole.

(Nag Hammadi)

YEHSUA

When You Die

The information that follows pertains to what we would anticipate happening when we pass away. The majority of people are quite uncomfortable talking about death, which is unfortunate because a great number of souls who are going through the process of dying are very confused about it because they do not know what to anticipate. Let's face it, we all have to die. Considering that we do not know when we are going to pass away, I felt it would be a good idea to find out what it is before it is too late to do something about it now. It does not matter to me if I am an agnostic, a secular, a strongly religious, or an atheist; the knowledge that I am going to deliver is going to be the same regardless of my beliefs. Because of our views, mother nature has been carrying out the process of death for millions of years, and she is not going to modify it because of our beliefs. The process of death is a very natural process. As a result, this is expected to be the case. The realisation that there is no such thing as death is the first thing that many people come to terms with. However, those who believe that death is the complete and entire loss of consciousness or awareness will have to come to terms with the truth that life continues after the physical death, and death is not the end that many people had anticipated or expected it to be. We will still have a body when we pass away, which is the next thing that will come to your mind. Rather than being a physical body composed of cells, it is a spiritual body composed of spiritual particles than a physical body. When compared to the previous body, this new body has a fairly similar sensation. There are some instances in which this spiritual body can even be younger and more attractive than the one we experienced previously. Another factor that will open our eyes is the fact that we cannot conceal anything from anyone. Every single one of our ideas, feelings, and wants, as well as other things, are now plainly visible to everyone. Our soul garment, which is often referred to as our aura, is where they are reflected. Another wonder is that, for the most part, we have not really changed much through the process of dying. Our personalities, traits, opinions, and the majority of our beliefs are entirely intact, whether they have changed for the better or for the worst. Everyone who had the expectation that they would be more knowledgeable or more enlightened after they pass away will be let down. On the other hand, all of our deep needs, cravings, addictions, habits, obsessions, or substance abuses will still be with us on the other side, and they will be felt intensely. This is the next important realisation that will open our eyes. The issue is that we do not own a physical body that can fulfil their needs like we once did. The second thing that hits us like an enormous amount of stones is the realisation that the majority of the things we have been pursuing on this planet are not significant. This includes things like personal accomplishments, prestige, careers, accumulating things, fame, recognition, and so on. They are no longer significant, and the only thing that truly matters is the extent to which we have loved, served, and forgave those around us during our lifetimes. The next thing that will catch your attention is the fact that, in the majority of instances, beings of light, which we also refer to as angels, will greet us and assist us in adjusting to the new place where we will be residing. However, in order for this to take place, we must either grant them permission or demonstrate that we are willing to do so. There is no reason to be afraid of approaching them. In order to assist and direct us, they are here. The second thing that will amaze your mind is the fact that in many instances, we will also be greeted by loved ones who have passed away in the past, such as our spouses, friends, relatives, and other people. A reunion like this is typically a very happy occasion, and it is possible that we will even be greeted by our dogs or any other animal with whom we shared a very strong connection throughout our existence. The second thing that will amaze your mind is the fact that there will be no dancing about the throne of God, growing wings, sitting on clouds, or strumming hearts. It is possible that the new spiritual world that we have entered appears to be remarkably similar to the one that we have left behind, and it provides a wide range of activities that can help our souls advance in their development. One further thing that will open your eyes is the fact that there is no such thing as an endless hell, damnation, or the ultimate day of judgement. These ideas were conceived by human beings who desired to exert control over other people through the use of fear. The truth is that it is of no consequence whether you believe any of the information that I have revealed with you because you will, at some point in the future, discover it for yourself. The only thing I would like you to keep in mind is that when we make the transition that we refer to as death, we should keep an eye out for those light beings. They are there to assist us and to guide us, and we must not be intimidated by their bright light. Instead, we should not be afraid to approach them and simply ask them to take us to our new dwelling.

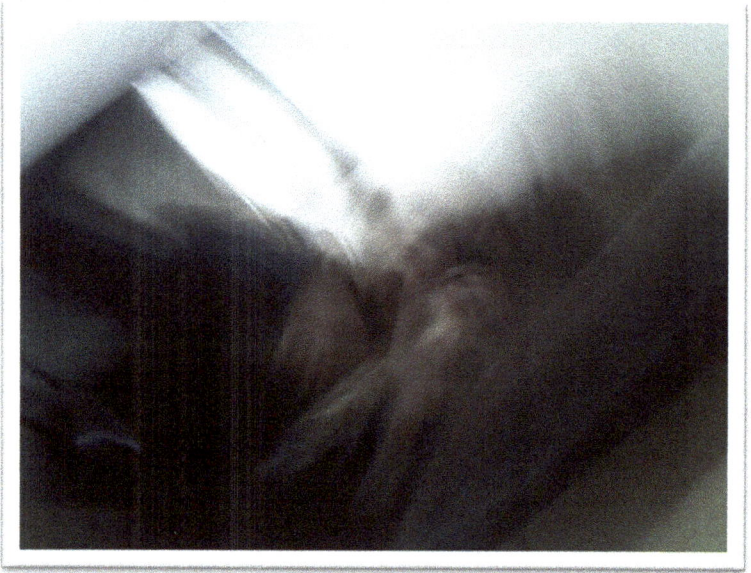

This heaven will pass away, and the one above it will pass away. The dead are not alive, and the living will not die.

(Nag Hammadi)

YESHUA

God Within

When Yeshua claimed that the Kingdom of Yahweh is truly inside us, what did he imply by that statement as well? How is that even possible? It is possible that you will find this to be quite interesting. To begin, I will discuss the seven-dimensional absolute reality, which is our genuine home and the place from which we all originated. The One Law is a profound silence that extends all the way down to the depths of the All being Yahweh. Within the luminous ocean of pure consciousness, which is also referred to as Yahweh's Spirit, there is now a profound calm that continues on forever. Producing an unlimited number of forms and phenomena through morphing. All energy and vibrations, which we humans also refer to as the All Being, the rules or powers of Yahweh, pure wisdom, and finally the pure Cosmic Eternal Love, are included in this. The One True Law Yahweh is made up of an infinite number of aspects of consciousness, which are various degrees of consciousness. These are the spiritual life forms, minerals, plants, animals, and other species of nature that are guided to the next higher degrees of consciousness by the Creator Yahweh, who is also known as the Spirit of evolution. Therefore, the absolute reality is a condition of perpetual motion that is exponential, and it is also characterised by continuous expansion and changes. It includes all of the spiritual universes, including all of the galaxies and stars, as well as their countless phases or degrees of evolution, beginning with the mineral kingdom and progressing all the way up to the perfect and eternal spirit beings, also known as angelic beings. Each of these beings is endowed by divinity with their own free will. In this place, the absolute reality, all of these occurrences and stages of the evolution of awareness coexist harmoniously with one another. As a single entity. Also, in complete accord. Within this heavenly fullness and richness, there are no deficiencies, no problems, no disputes, no illnesses, and no destructions. This sea of holy light is devoid of shadows; rather, it is characterised by a gradual and rhythmic progression. Pertaining to the many different manifestations of life or consciousness. Expressions of divine love are another term that might be used. In this place, every different kind of life is a manifestation of Yahweh, the Spirit of Yahweh. In addition to being in the form of life, as He does on earth, Yahweh is also present in every kind of life that exists in this absolute reality. He is self-aware and knows himself in the myriad of uncountable phenomena that are the result of creation. It is for this reason that we might also refer to it as absolute consciousness. There are multiple states of consciousness that are projected onto the world. Due to the fact that we have all been these magnificent spirit beings at one point in time, this is our true home. Therefore, why aren't we there any longer? What is the best way for us to enter our gloomy and heavy three-dimensionality? As we have seen, the gift of free will was one of the gifts that was bestowed upon these beautiful spirit beings in the absolute reality. At the beginning of creation, there was a sizeable number of perfect spirit beings who had made use of this ability and had made the decision to depart from this reality in order to construct their own creation. This rebellion of spirit beings was referred to as an exodus of spirit beings in the scriptures. There were several reasons for this rebellion. An angelic fall from grace. In his well-known version of the parable of the prodigal son, Yeshua makes reference to this significant occurrence. Regarding this particular instance, the father, who was a wealthy landowner, did not interfere with his son's desire or free will to leave his house. Even more, he handed over his inheritance to his son so that he may begin his new life in the world. This is a description of the actual events that took place when these countless angels travelled away from the pristine heavens. For the sake of getting their latest endeavour on the ground, they were provided with a set quantity of energy or light ether; nevertheless, things quickly went from bad to worse as they started arguing and fighting with one another. They began to establish their own relative or temporary reality, and along with it came the concepts of time and space, the domain of difference and opposites, and the law of cause and effect. Some of them found themselves in the lowest three-dimensional realm of matter, which is nothing but transformed down aspects of consciousness as the loaned energy depleted more and more. These fallen spirit beings experienced a sense of lack and scarcity for the very first time, which was completely opposite to the absolute reality, which is the fullness and abundance of Yahweh. As they fell further and further away from the pure heavens, their souls became more and more burdened with what we now refer to as karmic burdens. Over the course of aeons of time, their garments crystallised more and more until they found themselves in the lowest three-dimensional realm of matter. Because of this fear for survival, these beings have been involved in a never-ending cycle of conflicts, quarrels, theft, wars, murder, and other violent acts that continue to this day. All in the sake of power, energy, and control. The fact that we suffer, experience fear, rage, loneliness, and illness is explained by the fact that they are all the results of our own unloving thoughts, words, and acts, which we carried out of ignorance against our own highest. In point of fact, this fleeting reality is small, comparable to a grain of sand when compared to the expanse of a wide desert, which relates to the enormous, unlimited, immeasurable, and endless absolute reality. At some point in the future, when all of these fallen angels have returned to their homes, it will be absorbed back into the absolute reality. Once more, this is the most significant aspect of Yeshua's parable, which is about the homecoming of the prodigal son. In this part of the story, the father, who is delighted and loving, welcomes his son back home. It is time to proceed to the next level. Everyone has told us that everything may be found in everything. In the same way that the smallest portion is present in everything, the essence of everything may be found in the smallest part. Indeed, this immense reality, in addition to this temporal reality, is present in each and every atom, in each and every form of life, and yes, even in you and me. Yeshua said that the entire Kingdom of Yahweh is contained within each and every one of us, and he referred to our physical bodies as the temple of the Kingdom of Yahweh. At the seventh Energy Centre, the gateways to this inner endless kingdom lie at the very heart of what it means to be there. The holy stream of life runs down the spine and through all of the energy centres of our body, nourishing every organ and cell as it does so. This allows us to completely submerge ourselves in the love that is flowing via this stream. When we pray or meditate, we are able to experience the profound calm and fullness of Yahweh flooding into us. This provides us with a profound inner peace that the rest of the world does not know. We will lose all of the power that the outside world has over us because there is nothing more powerful than Yahweh, and there is nothing more powerful than love, and we are love because of His love. As we are surrounded and penetrated by the flow of life, we consciously acknowledge the life that is already present inside us. During this time, Yahweh directs our steps. Because His breath is also our breath, we are able to sense it. After we have discovered the inner Kingdom of Yahweh within ourselves, his love and power permeate each and every organ and cell of our bodies. In light of the fact that the outer world is really a relative universe consisting of temporary thought patterns that are projected, we start to live from the inside out. The Lord is everywhere at once. The assertion that Yahweh is in us and that we are in Yahweh is a powerful affirmation. Without Yahweh, it is impossible to be apart from him. In addition, we are not distinct from any other individual because the essence of each and every person and thing is contained within us. We will eventually raise our vibration and be attracted back to the Absolute reality, and we will be once again one of the eternal perfect Spirit beings in our true home. This will happen once we make use of our own free will and with the assistance of the Christ spark that is near our heart, which is both empowering and transformative, we will purify our soul step by step. As we make our way towards the divine, the Eternal, the driving force behind our journey is our profound need to get back home.

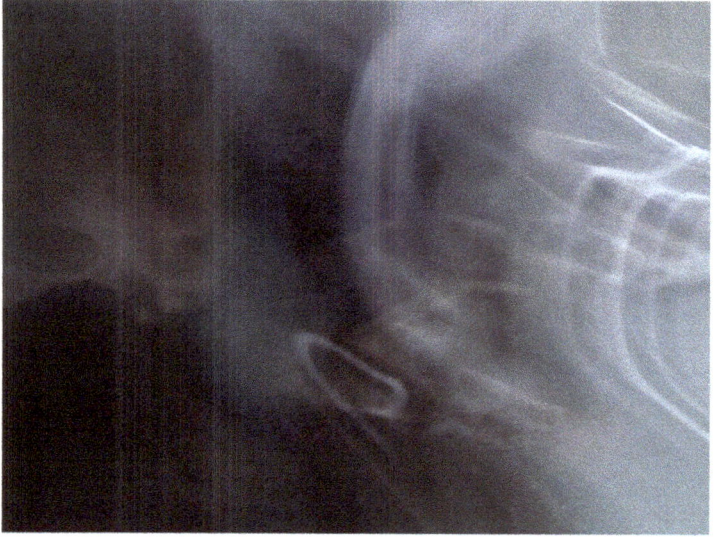

Do you not know that your bodies are temples of the Holy Spirit, who is in you, whom you have received from God? You are not your own.

(1 Corinthians 6:19)

YESHUA

How To Reach Heaven

For the reason that this is the only life we have, some people argue that we should make the most of it. Contrary to popular belief, that is not the case. You and I are immortal cosmic beings of infinity who have only spent a very brief length of time here on planet Earth. This is due to the fact that Earth is nothing but a place of learning and is comparable to any institution where we are required to learn. The duration is limited and typically concludes with graduation, which we commonly refer to as death. This is the moment when our soul departs from the physical body and returns to the spiritual realm from which we had originally originated. The manner in which we have spent our lives and mastered the lessons we have learned here on earth is the sole determining factor in whether or not we will graduate. Do we have a strong desire to worship our egos, or have we made use of our time to grow more loving and nicer to one another? As we prepare to leave our physical bodies behind, the way in which we have lived our lives on earth will dictate what we can anticipate. The events that take place after a person dies and in the time that follows are therefore unique to each individual. How about we take a more in-depth look at that? Every single object is energy, as we are aware. For example, our thoughts and words are considered to be types of vibrational energy. They use visuals to convey the information they have. Although we may not be aware of it, we are only able to think in terms of visuals and images. Not only are all of our thoughts about unresolved issues in our life's pictorial vibrations, but they are also stored in our souls, which are located in the repository planets of the material and semi-material universes. However, the most important thing is that these vibrations are also stored in our subconscious, and these images are pictures that will become our initial external reality when we passed away. Upon our passing, we will be confronted by them. If, however, our physical bodies were not there to protect us. That can be a little anxious at times. The quality of our afterlife will be affected by any issues that we have not resolved in this physical life that we are doing right now. Because of this, it is of the utmost importance that we deal with our shadows right now, as Carl Jung makes reference to our unconscious side, which is comprised of unresolved inner conflicts, if we deal with them right now. Through conscious effort, we have the ability to alter our vibration and attract ourselves to realms that are more sophisticated, joyful, and enriching to our lives. Since everything in this place is powered by positive energy, which includes love, joy, and bliss. Who, after all, would regret going back to such place? Our origins can be traced back to that origin. After our physical bodies have passed away, let us ask ourselves, where do we believe our soul will go? In accordance with the spiritual rule of gravitation, which states that "like attracts like," also known as the law of attraction, our soul may only travel to a corresponding level or planet of purification to corresponding souls. Once there, it will congregate with individuals who share the same interests and objectives. Either in the upper spiritual worlds from whence we originally originated, in the lower end darker astral spheres, or even on earth as a soul that is connected to the earth, this can take place. Because of this, we are able to assert that the manner in which a person has lived is the same manner in which his soul will continue to feel and behave in the afterlife. It is a nice thing to know that we have the ability to dramatically affect the kind of life we will have after death if we make the most of the time we have left on this planet. If we want to attract the higher levels of purification, what are some things that we may do from this point forward to bring our soul into a higher vibration? This is a straightforward response that we have been told numerous times before. It is the advice that Yeshua offered to us two thousand years ago, and if we had listened to it, I believe that this world would have been transformed into a paradise. Love is the only thing that is recommended, other than that. This is both straightforward and uncomplicated. It has always been our insecure ego that has been opposed to this love thing. It has always wanted to be in charge and select who is deserving of our love and who is not, including ourselves. On the other hand, if we were to focus solely on love, everything else would fall into place. Whenever we were aware of our flaws, our darkness, and the weight that we carry on our souls, we would always take a look at them and tackle them. Remorse would be something that we would not hesitate to feel, and we would ask for forgiveness, make amends, and stop engaging in undesirable behaviours or mental patterns. Without reservation, we would forgive those who have wronged us if we did love. It is no longer acceptable to harbour resentment towards any individual. Mostly due to the fact that it would link the spirit of the person to us in the hereafter and in subsequent lifetimes until forgiveness is granted if we truly loved whoever we were. We would liberate ourselves from that which ties us to this reality, whether it be somebody or something. So that we can triumph over the negative energies that we have created in this or previous lifetimes, Yahweh bestows upon us each day his great energy. In order to change our negative energy into good energy, we would make use of the God-filled flame of the Divine Christ, which is located in the fourth energy centre or chakra. We would be honouring the golden rule, the ten commandments, and the Sermon on the Mount

127

if we truly loved one another. If we loved completely, we would not hurt anybody or anything. The words "love," "Yahweh," "your father above all else," and "your neighbour as yourself" would finally be put into practice. If we were to only love one another, without any other considerations. Our soul would be elevated, and we would also want to think about providing silent service to other people, in which we put them first without taking credit for it. This is because the most profound kind of love is service, and our mission is to live a life of joyous service to other people. Love is the only thing that is recommended to us by the divine powers that are present in us and all around us. They are here to assist us in achieving our objective, which is to arrive at our eternal home of light, peace, and love! The kind of existence that we shall have in the afterlife is going to be determined by us. That there are no riddles surrounding the topic of death is something that the spiritual world wants us to be aware of. It provides us with clear answers to all of the questions that we might have, such as how to talk to someone who is dying, the death of a child, suicide, sorrow, and grief. The planet of cleansing, karma, and a great deal more, as well as burial or cremation.

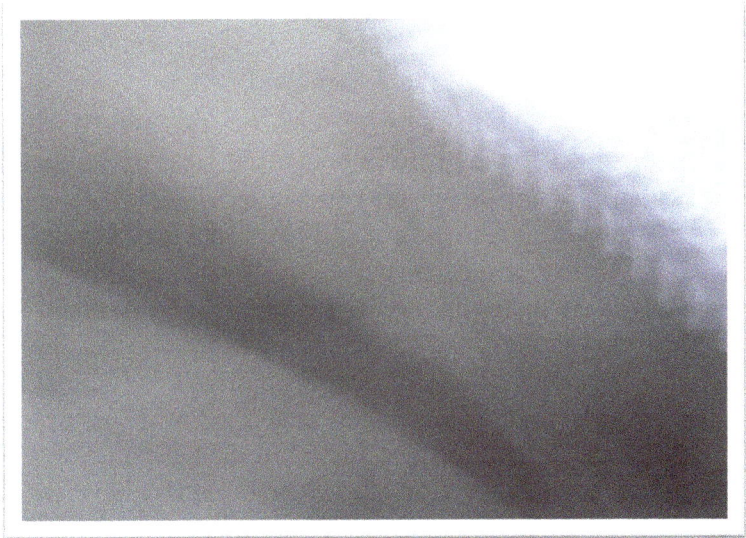

"Blessed is he who will stand at the beginning and he will know the end, and he will not taste death."

(Gospel of Thomas)

YESHUA

The Truth About the Ten Commandments

The word "commandment" can be the source of the problem. Everyone dislikes being told what to do. As soon as someone tells us what to do, we rebel against it, and we look for methods to get out of doing what they have told us to do. Consequently, over the course of time, people most likely considered these ten rules to be archaic and unworkable. Because Yogananda was an outsider, he was able to examine these ten commandments with great care and come to the conclusion that they were completely incorrect. In point of fact, these are the ten guidelines that will always lead to happiness. When we examine these and the commandments through the lens of this information. We are able to recognise the profound reality that these are, in fact, the rules that govern happiness, profound joy, harmony, and freedom. In the first one, "I am the Lord your God," let us take a look at it. You are not allowed to worship any other gods besides me. In this passage, God makes it abundantly clear to us how close he is to us and that we can approach him with everything that is troubling us in order to find genuine happiness. He encourages us to not bind ourselves to external objects or to other people, and he says this to us. It is also applicable to the things that we surround ourselves with. For the reason that all of our desires, passions, cravings, success, wealth, celebrity, or power are merely inadequate substitutes for the profound joy and contentment that we experience on the inside. Do you not think it is time for us to put these things away, just as a child would put away his toys, because we have simply outgrown them? "You shall not take the name of the Lord your God in vain," is the second commandment described in the New Testament. This serves as a gentle reminder to pray or worship Yahweh with a concentrated mind and heart, and to use his name with care and reverence. Additionally, it instructs us to become conscious of the fact that Yahweh is always present, as it is easy for us to become engrossed in our own personal illusions whenever we forget that. If you go through the day without giving it any attention or care, you will bring about turmoil and sorrow. Within each one of us, as well as in our neighbours, as well as in the animals, plants, and minerals that surround us, Yahweh is there. Yahweh is present across the entire world. It is through this knowledge, profound reverence, connection, and presence with Yahweh that we are able to experience happiness, as well as security and safety. The realisation that Yahweh is the sole rock to stand on and the only hold on which we can rely will come to each and every one of us sooner or later. "Observe the Sabbath day in order to keep it holy," is the focus of the third commandment. This is a really astute request to set aside one day of the week for the purpose of cultivating inner serenity and introspection, specifically a day in which we focus on developing our inner life rather than our outer life. In this place, we are able to disengage from the illusions of the world and regain our sense of ourselves, as well as our reason for being here and our destination. Being by oneself and in silence for a short period of time, and taking pleasure in the inner stillness, brings about mental healing and peace of mind after the chaotic six days that have just passed. The price of grandeur is to be found in solitude. Recharging our batteries through communication with Yahweh, the source of all existence, enables us to face the upcoming week with a sense of peace, power, and enjoyment. Because of this, it is in our best interest to keep one day separate for him, as it will be beneficial to both our mental and physical health. Within a short period of time, each day will eventually be a day of profound connection and inner communication with Yahweh. The fourth promise is to "Honour both your mother and your father." The very first persons we come into contact with are our parents. The representatives of Yahweh, who is the most powerful father, are these individuals. If we do not value and respect them, then how can we possibly love other people so much? In the process of coming to terms with who we are, our parents serve as the first mirrors we look at, reflecting our own selves back to us. Eventually, we will need to resolve any unloving connections we have with our parents and, naturally, with everyone else in order to properly enjoy a life of permanent inner peace and happiness over our lifetimes. "Thou shalt not kill," comes from the fifth commandment. The fact that we are unable to generate new life is brought to our attention by this. Because of this, we do not have the authority to put an end to the incarnations of other people, even our own. The principle of cause and effect would be put into practice as a result of this. The proverb "He who will take up the sword will die by the sword" is something that each and every one of us has heard. Therefore, an attitude of profound appreciation for all kinds of life, not just humans, is necessary for pleasure. Certainly, this also includes the obligation to refrain from killing the creatures that are our younger siblings and cousins. Committing adultery is forbidden, according to the sixth commandment. In point of fact, it is always our thoughts that come first. There has been a disintegration of trust and allegiance. When it comes to the foundation of a marriage or partnership, why is it significant that commitment, respect, and honesty are so important? Because they make it possible for both partners to grow in terms of personal freedom and the unfolding of their contributions and gifts that are unique to them. Isn't that what people call happiness? Therefore, "you shall not steal" is the seventh commandment. It is always the mind that is the starting point for theft, when we start to crave what other people have. Karma is always created when we take something away from someone, whether it is their property, their love, their peace, or any other item. This causes us to get entangled with our victim, often for many future incarnations. Nevertheless, we are also capable of stealing time and energy from our neighbour when, for example, we engage in unimportant conversations with him in an attempt to impose our will or our opinions on other people. The bitter lessons that we learned from it will always come back to us. To be happy, therefore, is to be conscious of the fact that Yahweh, the whole of life, resides within each an individual. Instead than lusting after the things that other people have, why not let our inner riches shine through? It is written in the eighth commandment that "you shall not bear false witness against thy neighbour." Have any of us ever given any thought to the ease with which we might cause harm to another person by distorting the facts through our idle chatter and gossip? On the other hand, giving false witness also involves showering our neighbour with flowery words in order to acquire something for ourselves. This is a form of flattery against our neighbour. It is true that everything is energy, and any negative energy that we send out into the world through our thoughts, words, and actions will eventually come back to confront us. Therefore, whether or not we tell the truth about other people, whether or not we lie about them, affects the level of enjoyment that we experience in our lives. A commandment number nine. Both the tenth commitment, which states, "You shall not covet your neighbour's wife, servant, handmaid, or anything else that your neighbour has," and the tenth commitment, which states, "You should not covet your neighbour's house." If we have a desire for the belongings of other people, it indicates that we are searching for satisfaction and fulfilment in the world outside of ourselves. On the contrary, this is a source of dissatisfaction, sorrow, and unhappiness that is guaranteed to be present within us. These needs and wishes are the product of our five senses, which are always pulling us into the outside world. This pulls us away from the greatest treasure of all that is within us, which is Yahweh, who is the fullness and who always gives us everything we require. Once we have a clear understanding of the distinction between what we want and what we require, we can easily arrive to a state of illumination. Make sure you don't forget to question yourself, "How can I tell that I don't require what I want?" No, I do not possess it. There you have it: wisdom. When we look at these ten commandments through the lens of freedom, profound joy, and happiness, don't you think they become much more applicable and even inviting?

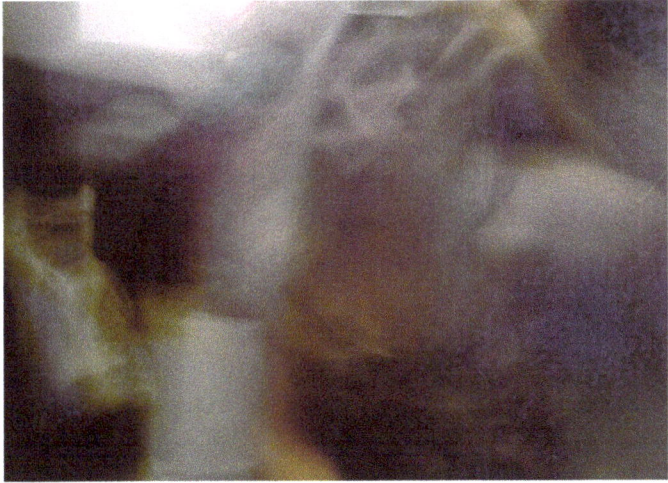

Jesus said, "I took my stand in the midst of the world, and in flesh I appeared to them. I found them all drunk, and I did not find any of them thirsty. My soul ached for the children of humanity, because they are blind in their hearts and do not see, for they came into the world empty, and they also seek to depart from the world empty. But meanwhile they are drunk. When they shake off their wine, then they will change their ways."

(Nag Hammadi)

YESHUA

Sermon on the Mount

The divine being provided us with three suggestions regarding how we ought to live our lives. The golden rule, the ten commandments, and the Sermon on the Mount were the three things that were mentioned. Many people are not familiar with the teachings and life of Yeshua, and even many Christians rarely remember the Sermon on the Mount, if they have ever read it at all. Despite this, even though the Sermon on the Mount is the way that leads to Yahweh, the path of perfection, many people are not familiar with it. Approximately two thousand years ago, Yeshua imparted this instruction. After it was memorised, recounted, retold, retold, and retold, written down, copied, and recopied, and translated, the majority of scholars believe that it was written down in the Gospel of Matthew one hundred years later. There are several minor adjustments, variants, and changes that have been included into the text. Despite the fact that the text that we find in the Bible is not even close to being real, the deeper meaning and the true substance of the Sermon on the Mount are still applicable to us today. I would like to remind us of the most important teachings that we can find in Christ's Sermon on the Mount. The additional explanations that I give with each teaching are taken from a book in which Yeshua himself elaborated, explained, and even corrected the sentences. I share these explanations with you. "Those who are poor are blessed in the spirit, for it is theirs that the kingdom of heaven belongs to!" It is Yeshua who clarifies the word. What is meant by the term "poor" is not the ownership of worldly stuff; rather, it refers to individuals who do not endeavour to acquire personal possessions and who do not hoard goods. Their inner wealth is a life in Yahweh, a life for Yahweh and for their neighbour. This is their ultimate goal. Yeshua emphasises that individuals who are in mourning are blessed because they will thereafter be comforted. It is not Yahweh who is responsible for the suffering of man. Those who are able to suffer their loss without condemning their neighbour, who are able to recognise their own shortcomings and weaknesses in the midst of their grief, who are able to repent of those shortcomings, and who pray for pardon and forgiveness from Yahweh will be granted mercy. The meek will be blessed since they will be the ones to possess the earth. Yeshua explains that another characteristic of love is that it is gentle, humble, and kind. Love is also selfless. Both wisdom and strength are contained inside these. "Blessed are those who hunger and thirst for righteousness, for they shall be completely satisfied," the Bible says. According to Yeshua, If you make it a habit to think and live in a constructive manner, you will very gradually transform into a person who exudes righteousness. At that time, you will bring the righteousness that Yahweh has for the world into existence. "Those who are merciful will be blessed, for they will be granted mercy." The explanation that Yeshua gives is that anybody who makes an effort to be merciful will eventually achieve kindness. Those who have a pure heart will be blessed, since they will be able to see Yahweh. It is because they have once again become representations of the Heavenly Father that Yeshua explains. Gentleness and humility seem to emanate from their heart, which is pure and meek. Blessed are those who work to bring about peace, for they will be referred to as children of Yahweh. It is explained by Yeshua that individuals who maintain peace will likewise bring true peace to this earth because they have achieved peace within themselves. According to the explanation that Yeshua provides, "Blessed are those who suffer persecution for the sake of righteousness, for theirs is the Kingdom of Yahweh." The people who followed me were not respected by the people of the world because they looked down on me as the Messiah. Recognise that I was also looked down upon by them. When Yeshua says, "Woe unto you who are rich, for you have received your consolation in this life," he is referring to a person who is wealthy in material possessions and has realised that his wealth is a gift that he has received from Yahweh. The purpose of this wealth is to bring it into the great whole for the well-being of everyone, and to administer it in the appropriate manner for everyone. Is the individual who brings the principles of equality, freedom, unity, and brotherhood into tangible form. Because of this, a balance will be gradually achieved, and an upper middle class will be created for all those individuals who are prepared to labour, pray, and fulfil the law without seeking personal gain. "To those who are satisfied, I say, woe to you, for you will hunger." Yeshua argues that the prosperous and contented folks who simply fill their own barns are heartless about their situation. Those who laugh at this time will be the ones to sorrow and weep in the future. The explanation that Yeshua gives is that whomever judges and condemns his neighbour, laughs at him, scorns and ridicules him, judges, condemns, laughs at, scorns and ridicules me, the Christ. Yeshua emphasises that everyone who commits a sin against even the least of my brothers acts in violation of the law of life and will be forced to endure the consequences of their actions. According to Yeshua, "Woe unto you when all men speak well of you, for so did their forefathers with the false prophets." If you flatter your fellow man in such a way that he praises you and holds you in respect, then you are similar to counterfeiters, who, for the sake of their own gain, pay and pay for a false coin. "Reconcile with your brother," Yeshua says, explaining that the mandate to forgive and beg for forgiveness will continue to be valid until all that is not in conformity with the everlasting rules is atoned for and cleared up. As Yeshua instructs, "Reach agreement with your adversary quickly while you are still on your way with him." Do not let the evil that you committed against your neighbour to remain unresolved. It is imperative that you eliminate this matter as quickly as possible, as he is still accompanying you on your journey through life in this earthly existence. On the other hand, I tell you to love your adversaries and to be kind to those who despise you. The explanation that Yeshua gives is that every individual ought to recognise his neighbour, his brother and sister, in every one of his fellow men. It is important to recognise your neighbour and make an effort to love him without condition, even if he appears to be your adversary. The person who appears to be your adversary can even serve as a useful mirror for self-recognition. Because if something in your neighbour offends you, it is likely that the same or something similar is present in you as well. "Because if you love those who love you, will you receive any reward for your actions?" Therefore, Yeshua teaches that you should welcome and receive your neighbour in your heart, even if he does not love you, even if he does not aid you, and even if he ignores you love him. Be as unselfish as the sun is in its love for the earth and appreciate every single person and every single being. "And if you want something that will bring grief and suffering to another person, rip it out of your heart," that was said by Yeshua. Yeshua adds that if you consequently have to bear anguish and sorrow, you should not blame your neighbour for your position. He says, "Be therefore perfect as the Father in heaven is perfect." In contrast to your neighbour, you are the one who is responsible for creating it. Your anguish and your sadness are the seeds that have germinated within your soul, and they manifest themselves in or on your body as harvest. "In order to maintain the confidentiality of your alms, you must ensure that your left hand is not aware of what your right hand is doing." Yeshua argues that a person who does good for his neighbour only when the neighbour expresses gratitude to him for it and praises his good works has not done it for his neighbour but rather for himself. Yeshua continues, "But when you pray, go into your chamber." When you pray, you should retreat into a peaceful room and immerse yourself deeply into your inner being. This is because the spirit of the father, whose temple you are, resides inside you. The more deeply a person delves into the divine understanding, the more they should be recognised. It is more likely that he will pray with fewer words. Even though they are brief, his prayers are extremely powerful because the word reflects the power that is lived. In his explanation, Yehsua says, "Do not murmur like hopeless people; do not mourn your dead individuals!" The life of the soul is not the same as the life of the body, the life, or the temporal. In order to cleanse and settle in the temporal what it had done upon itself in many worldly clothing, the soul took on body for the brief period of time that it was able to do so. The human being on earth and the soul in the realms of purification will one day be led to the decision to serve Yahweh or mammon, to be for Yahweh or against Yahweh. Yeshua adds that "no one can serve two masters," and that this decision will be made in the same way. According to Yeshua, "Therefore, do not be concerned about the evil of tomorrow's," only the individual who does not entrust himself to Yahweh, allowing the days to pass without making use of them, is the one who is concerned about the problems that will occur tomorrow. Plan each day, and make sure that you plan it well. Also, make sure that you give yourself time for some introspection so that you can find some inner stillness and think about your life and plans again and again. You should not evaluate yourself because you will not be judged. Yeshua teaches that you are your own judge, and that your negative thoughts, words, and actions contribute to that judgement. In the same way that you treat your neighbour in your thoughts, words, and actions, you will eventually fear how you treat yourself. I am curious as to how you are able to perceive the splinter in your brother's eye while at the same time being unaware of the beam that is in your own eye. Therefore, anyone speaks badly about his fellow man and who slanders and denigrates him is not aware of his own shortcomings, as Yeshua teaches. The individual who is able to first get rid of his own shortcomings is also able to assist his neighbour. It is for this reason that anyone who criticises his brother's shortcomings and, in doing so, fails to recognise the positive aspects of his own behaviour is a hypocrite. In the same way that you would like other people to treat you, you should treat them in the same manner. Yeshua says that it is against the law to coerce, from a position of expectation, your fellow men into acts, words, or specific behaviours that you would not be willing to engage in if you were in the same situation. Whatever it is that you do not want to happen to you, you should also avoid doing to any of your neighbours, since everything that you send out into the world comes back to you. The reason for this is that you should evaluate your thoughts and watch what you say. I make a comparison between the person who listens to these words of mine and acts upon them and a wise person who constructed his home firmly on a rock.

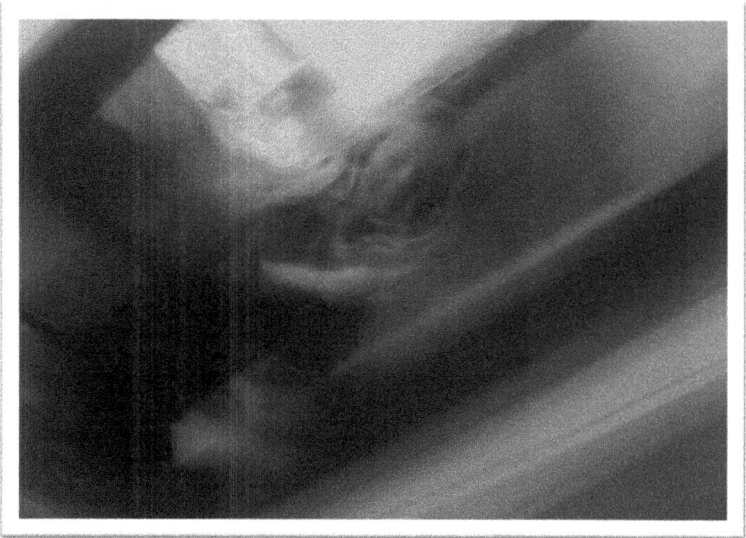

"I am the Alpha and the Omega, the first and the last, the beginning and the end."

(Revelation 22:13)

.

Milton Keynes UK
Ingram Content Group UK Ltd.
UKHW020836061224
452240UK00009B/540

9 781917 601290